Recollections o_ JAZZ

in Bristol

compiled by

DAVE HIBBERD

"My Kind of Town"

A TRIBUTE EDITION

VOLUME 1

NEW ORLEANS TO MAINSTREAM

FIDUCIA PRESS

Recollections of
JAZZ
in Bristol
MY KIND OF TOWN

Compiled by

Dave Hibberd

A TRIBUTE EDITION

Foreword by Acker Bilk

Front Cover by Beryl Cook

Editors Roy Gallop Tess Green Ken Griffiths

Book Design Roy Gallop, Ken Griffiths and Rosie Tomlinson

Typing Services Leighanne Gough and Joanne Howard

Photographic Processing John Brewer

First impression 2000

FIDUCIA PRESS 2009

ISBN 978 0 946217 33 5

Printed in Great Britain by Doveton Press Ltd., of Bristol.

CONTENTS

Front Cover. A painting by Beryl Cook of the Dave Collett Trio at The White Horse Bedminster.

Back Cover Montage Top. Back Row L to R: Geoff Nichols, Ray Bush, Mike Hitchings, Step Whitehead, Roy Smith, Clive Whittingham, Acker Bilk, Gerry Bath, Alan Scott, John Gill, Nick Cooper, Frank Fennell, Dave Creech and Barry Back.

Middle Row. L to R: Andy Leggett, Ian (Flurge) Appleyard, Tony Osborne, Geoff Roberts and Norman Hill.

Front Row. L to R: Alan Taylor, Roger Bennett, Don Burnell, Les Drake, Mike Cocks and Geoff Weldrake.

Back Cover Montage Bottom. L to R: Sammi Brown, Angie Masterson, Eiri Thrasher, Teri Leggatt, Hannah Wedlock, Min Newman, Pat Purchase, Kate McNab and Pam Coster.

Title Page. Dave Hibberd and his wife Jean at a New Chicagoans gig, at the Arnos Court Hotel in 1967.

FOREWORD

From 1950 to 1957 most of my playing was done in and around Bristol. This shaped my clarinet style and ultimately the shape of my life. During this period I made my first radio broadcasts and TV appearances for the late and much missed Brian Patten. I also cut my first commercial records and embarked on my first international tour.

Venues included the Crown and Dove, The Foundry Inn and the Ship on Redcliff Hill, all of which have since been flattened and built on at least once.

Much later I was able to open the Granary as a 7 night a week jazz venue, which featured numerous world famous jazzers. I am delighted that this book has been written by musicians who actually played jazz in Bristol over the last half century. Like all the best ideas you wonder why no-one has thought of it before. If they had though, this book would have been much shorter because the Bristol Jazz Scene is both healthy and ongoing.

Cheers!
Adrian Bill

This book is dedicated to my wife Jean and our daughter Lisa in appreciation of their work for the Bristol Jazz Society.

INTRODUCTION

This book does not attempt to be a formal history of jazz in Bristol, but a story of jazz in and around the city, told by those people who made it. It is not possible to include every jazz musician but it is hoped that from those that have contributed a picture will emerge of the vibrancy, commitment, musicianship and sheer enjoyment engendered by the musicians and their followers over the past fifty years.

The musicians' stories are told in many voices and therefore there will be many points of view. Memories of the same event are described somewhat differently and from another perspective. There will be contradictions and confirmations about what happened, where and when, but it will be told in a way that cannot be found in a formal record.

This volume cannot claim to be comprehensive. Jazz in Bristol was an ever changing and complex scene. A lot of information has already been lost with the passing of musicians and band managers. Very little has been written down, mainly because jazz musicians played rather than kept literary diaries. However, before too much was further lost to time it was felt that some memories, both written and photographic should be recorded here.

Places are as evocative as time and the many venues mentioned will no doubt recall some happy occasions; meetings with people that gave much enjoyment, long lasting friendships and romantic involvements, some that resulted in marriages. Jazz like other musical forms tend to play on the emotions.

The compass of this volume is the more traditional styles of the music, New Orleans to Mainstream. The Big Bands and Modern Jazz in all it's various forms must wait for volume 2.

Finally, as readers will notice as they read on, that without the contributors there would be no book, so to use that well-worn phrase, without them none of this would have been possible.

Dave Hibberd

THE 1940s

THE AVON CITIES A LONG HISTORY

In the beginning.....

It was a foggy evening in November 1949 in a flat above a sweet shop in Redcliffe Street. A disparate collection of teenagers talked seriously of forming a jazz band to play 'real' jazz, rather than the ersatz music of Harry James, Sid Philips, Ted Heath and Charlie Parker. The sum total of ignorance among them was monumental but their intentions were honourable. Some of these young men became the founder members of what was to become one of the great permanent institutions of post war British jazz.

The original line-up was: Ray Bush, clarinet; John Macey, banjo, were both motor mechanics; Basil Wright from Bath, on drums, was an ex-merchant seaman; Conrad Gillespie, known rather perjoratively as 'Diz', was a trombone player and student teacher. Geoff Nichols, trumpet, had just left school, and Glyn Wilcox on piano. Glyn was by far the most experienced of the group and regarded as something of a virtuoso by the rest of us; he was in his early twenties. This group formed the nucleus of the band.

Jazz bands were like football teams in those days, very much related to and identifying with their locality, so, as Glyn and Basil came from Bath and the rest from Bristol, Avon Cities Jazz Band seemed an appropriate name.

A week later, with a repertoire of about a dozen tunes the band (though not yet fully formed) played at the Newbridge Inn at Bath along with a quartet of architectural students from Bristol, which included Mike Hitchings playing clarinet and soprano sax, and Pat Beaghan on bass. Both agreed to join the band and the Avon Cities Jazz Band was complete.

A few weeks hence they played at the Bristol Arts Ball at the Grand Hotel, their first real 'gig'. Their first set consisted of all the tunes they knew and for their second set they played them once again. The Avons were in business.

The Fifties

In February 1950, someone discovered an empty hut in the grounds of the YWCA headquarters at the top of Great George Street, off Park Street, and the New Orleans Jazz Club was born, complete with membership cards, a constitution, and a regular club night on Friday evenings. No toilets, no bar, no amplification or cloakroom. Heating was provided by an old 'barrack room' type stove, lit early on winter evenings by 'Pop' Jones the ancient caretaker.

Every Friday for the next six years, the 'hut' was packed with the 'Jazz Youth' of Bristol, and meanwhile the band learnt its craft. King Oliver, Louis Armstrong, Jelly Roll Morton, Bunk Johnson and George Lewis were their idols as they memorised the jazz classics, and incidentally learnt also to play their instruments.

The band acquired a vocalist, Alan Tuckett, who belted out Bessie Smith and Ma Rainey blues choruses without the benefit of microphone or even megaphone. The hugely tall Jan Ridd replaced Glyn Wilcox at the piano and introduced the band to the future delights of mainstream jazz. Basil's brother, Malcolm, became the first (and probably last) left handed bass player, and John Macey's protégé, Jay Hawkings, added a second banjo to the rhythm section.

Christmas parties, quizzes, jazz lectures and heated discussions took place regularly, and the club was host to the original Ken Colyer Jazzmen (including Chris Barber, Lonnie Donegan and Monty Sunshine) for a memorable session.

In 1951 the band hired a coach, filled it with supporters (just like a football team) and travelled up to the Empress Hall at Earl's Court to take part in the first National Jazz Band Competition, where they came second, beating Barber, Mulligan, etc.

A National Service stint for Geoff Nichols from 1953 to 1955 produced further changes. Mike Hitchings led the band on soprano sax (as Roger Bennett, his pupil, was to do in later years with the

At the Foundry Inn, 1950: Jan Ridd, piano; Mike Hitchings, clarinet; Conrad (Diz) Gillespie, trombone; Ray Bush, clarinet; Geoff Nichols, trumpet; Basil Wright, drums; Jay Hawkins, banjo, and Malcolm Wright, bass.

Blue Notes) and John Skuse joined the band on trombone. Wayne Chandler replaced John Macey and Jay Hawkings on banjo, who had left to join the Acker Bilk band. John had now bought a double bass, well aware that a jazzer who not only owned a bass but could also play it accurately was in very short supply at that time. After his demobilisation Geoff played valve trombone for a short period while Mike bought a trombone and learnt how to play it within a few months. Geoff then returned to his original instrument and the front line was established which was to last for the next thirty years.

In 1956 Ray Bush formed the 'Avon Cities Skiffle' from within the band, to explore the hitherto neglected world of Black American Blues and folk music. Basil obtained a washboard and some thimbles, Mike taught himself to play the mandolin in a few days, Geoff borrowed the band bass for the sessions, while Ray and Wayne provided the guitar accompaniment for Ray's vocals. "Green Corn", "This Little Light of Mine", "Fisherman's Blues", "How Long Blues", etc, all came from Ray's collection of "Folkways" and "Library of Congress" recordings, and one of these was included as a 'filler' in a demo tape of the band which was sent to Decca in 1956.

As a result the first commercial records issued under the Avon Cities banner were two Extended Play '45s' by Ray Bush and the Avon Cities Skiffle, this time of some extracts from radio shows of the time.

The first L.P. by the full band was recorded at the famous Decca Studios at Broadhurst Gardens in Hempstead, and issued on their jazz label, Tempo, in 1957. The band have continued to record albums (and recently a CD) ever since.

In the late 1950s the band plus skiffle group made their first tours abroad, visiting Northern Ireland and Denmark. Concerts at the Royal Festival Hall, the Stoll Theatre and the Albert Hall established the band in the metropolis, as did their regular appearances at the 100 Club in Oxford Street.

The Sixties

The next ten years saw some fundamental changes in the band, not only in musical style, but also in club location and personnel.

Jan was the first to go - he apparently decided he'd had enough of the travelling, hassles, etc. In between "South Rampart Street Parade" and "Roll 'em Pete", he left during a concert on the end of Bognor Regis Pier in what seemed like a hurricane. After a while, John Critchinson, later to achieve fame in his own right as Ronnie Scott's pianist, joined the band and brought a breath of new musical air with him, as well as a lot of laughter (and some tears).

The brothers Wright left in the late 1950s, replaced by John Phipps on bass and Tim Ricketts on drums, the first import from the world of the dance band, and Tim also brought with him a whiff of the world of Damon Runyon; gambling, night clubs, wheeling and dealing, fast cars and fast girls were all part of Tim's world, and it was a world that was to re-emerge musically in the suite "Runyonland", which Geoff wrote and the Avon's created in 1985.

The Local Authority eventually discovered the deadly dangerous situation at the YWCA in 1957 and closed it down, from whence the club, now called The Avon Cities Club (the band had outgrown the style) moved to a vacant dance hall and night club known as the Worrall Rooms, off Blackboy Hill. Mike Bevan, one of the originals from Great George Street who had been managing the band since the early fifties, also ran the club. He was assisted by a club secretary and a bouncer/doorman called Dave Prowse, later to find fame and fortune as Darth Vadar in the "Star Wars" film. And, indeed help on the door was needed every Friday as a queue formed outside the club entrance to find an early seat at the club tables near the band. The band continued to try out different ways of playing jazz away from the tried and tested traditional formulae. Harmonized arrangements, non-jazz tunes and themes, 'swing' arrangements, all went to make up a typical Avon Cities session. During this residency the banjo

9

returned to the band in the ample shape of Frank Feeney, a recruit from the now-dying skiffle craze.

After the Worrall Rooms session, if the band packed up quickly enough, the midnight striptease at Lester's Club next door could be viewed - a pretty tame affair by today's standards, but really fast living in 1960. "Just in time for a quick late night beer" was the lame excuse for the rapid dumping of instruments into cases and the hurried trot to the side door of Lester's.

In 1963 the Avon's recorded four tracks for the Ace of Clubs label, to form part of a compilation LP of traditional jazz. This session featured a vocal by Chris Marlowe, who had succeeded Pam Coster and then Eve St. Clair as female band vocalist. Chris spent many years with the band, and only left to pursue a solo career as 'Sammi Brown.'

In the same year the Avon Cities club moved once again, this time to the centre of Bristol, to Carwardines basement in Baldwin Street. Still a 'dry' club, but providing very good coffee. A trio (modern usually) or a cabaret act performed during the band intervals in the Clipper Room under the stairs. The dancing took place in the main room, and, like the Worrall rooms, this was a dancing club. The Avon's responded to demand by introducing a blues and funk element into their programmes.

Dave Collett, who had left his own band in 1963 to join the Avons, was noted by the local press to be "the first jazz band pianist to use an electric piano, giving them a big lead in this field." The same paper ran an annual poll among its poll readers which regularly voted the Avon Cities as "top jazz group".

As well as regular appearances at jazz clubs in Southampton (Concorde), Birmingham (Waterworks), Nottingham (Dancing Slipper), London (100 Club), and Manchester (Bodega), etc, the Avons were still in demand for local university functions at the Victoria Rooms, though social and musical fashions were changing and the 3 guitar+3 chord

rock groups had arrived on the scene.

One of the more bizarre band appearances was at the Colston Hall in 1964 when they supported one of these new young groups - The Rolling Stones. The band also made an early TV appearance on "The Six Five Special", the "Top of the Pops" of the day.

Chris Pope joined the band on drums during their stay at Carwardines, having moved into Bristol from the Weymouth area. He has been with the band ever since, providing the rhythm section with a strength and swing to enable them to move into a different gear over the next ten years from straight ahead dixieland/mainstream to the more complex arrangements of the seventies.

In 1969 Acker Bilk opened his own 'dream' jazz club in a Victorian warehouse near to Redcliffe Bridge. It was called The Granary and the Avons played there every Friday for the next nine years until its closure as a jazz club in 1978. Bassist Clive Morton was spotted as part of the John Critchinson trio while playing an interval spot, and joined the band, succeeding Bernie Attridge who was to find his way to New Orleans and form a band there.

The Seventies

The combination of Nichols, Hitchings, Bush, Collett, Feeney, Morton and Pope, was a winning one, able to adapt and absorb many different musical ideas and styles while continuing to play the classic and mainstream jazz that they had cut their teeth on in the 1950s.

The Granary was a great place to hold a residency and many great names performed there, some with the Avon Cities as backing band; Charlie Shavers, Benny Carter, Muddy Waters, Ruby Braff, Tubby Hayes, NYJO, the Maynard Ferguson Big Band, Red Norvo, Humphrey Lyttelton, Champion Jack Dupree, plus many others bumped their heads on the low lintel as they emerged from the cupboard, laughingly known as 'the dressing room', onto the stage. Muddy

Waters not only bumped his head, but in doing so, all but lost his carefully situated hairpiece.

Members of the Duke Ellington and Count Basie bands dropped in for a late night taste after concerts at the Colston Hall (the sight of Johnny Hodges having a drink at the bar a few yards away could induce nervous exhaustion!), but these were exciting times, and the Granary was definitely the place to be at. It was also the first time the band was paid a wage for a residency, rather than a share of the take. This was quite a weight off the manager's mind, but also an added responsibility - to justify their continued employment.

The Avon Cities made four important LPs in the seventies, having moved from Decca to Joy Records. "Bristol Fashion" (later to be reissued by Decca) set the pattern with two Beatles arrangements ("Norwegian Wood" and "Hey Jude"), four originals from within the band and only "Grandpa's Spells" from the classic era.

In 1973, "Blue Funk" was issued, in which songs from the shows were featured, including ambitious arrangements of themes from "Jesus Christ Superstar", "Godspell" and "Hair", as well as Prokofiev and Joe Zavinul. The "Silver Collection" of 1974 (a twenty five year commemoration) was recorded in Bristol and further demonstrated the, by now, standard pattern of programme which the Avon Cities were presenting - arrangements of 'non-jazz' "Czar Paul". Vocals by Ray and Dave separately and together, which had replaced the once obligatory band vocalists of the early days. Not so pretty, but much more reliable. There was also a drum feature for Chris ("El Condor Pasa") and even an arrangement of a lesser known Joplin rag.

"Current AC" recorded in 1977 continued the same trend towards selecticism in all things, and included four original compositions, plus a Helen Reddy gospel song, sung by Dave, and even double-tracking to produce a Latin American percussion section on Ray's "Brazilian Bounce."

1977 also saw the TV transmission of the band with its own show in "Jazz on the Quay" - two half hour programmes recorded on a 'Union Jack' stage outside the Old Duke - a foretaste, perhaps, of the open air Duke festivals to come.

In 1978 the Granary closed as a jazz club. The Avon Cities played for the last night to a huge and emotional crowd but were soon after decorating yet another club of their own, this time at the Green Room at the bottom end of King Street. Mike Hitchings designed the stage decor, as he had done nearly thirty years before at their first club in Great George Street. Smaller than the Granary, with a small veranda of tables and chairs on one side, a long bar on the other and plenty of dancing space in the middle.

Once again the Avon Cities Club was in operation for members and guests every Friday evening, 8.30 - 11.00 pm. They welcomed various celebrities and some star musicians. Barry Humphries came in unrecognised one evening. Barry Foster closely observed and took instruction from Chris Pope, prior to appearing in "Born in the Gardens" at the Theatre Royal, which required him to play a set of drums on the stage. Yank Lawson, Digby Fairweather, Gene Connors, John Slaughter and Jim Galloway all appeared at the club as guest artists.

The Eighties Onwards

By now the band was settled into a sort of middle age routine, with a personnel which had not altered in ten years, still playing jazz gigs all over the country, plus the occasional TV and Radio appearances.

The Green Room was demolished in the early eighties to make way for a roundabout and the band moved fifty yards up King Street to Yesterdays, a very suitable venue for a jazz night spot - seats, tables, floor space and a 'jazz club' atmosphere. Fridays was reserved once again for the Avons and the band settled down to yet another residency, nearer still to the ever-beckoning Old Duke but still charging admission and providing punters with another hour of jazz after the Duke closed at 11.00 pm.

Ray Bush had been leader, clarinettist, vocalist, and band manager for so long that it came as a great shock when, in November 1983, he announced that he was about to emigrate to California to set up home with his American wife, Janice. An emergency meeting was held at Ray's home as "what to do?", Could he be replaced?, "Was it time to call it a day?", etc, etc', and it was Ray himself who suggested augmenting the band with a second reedman, to change the style once again in a new direction. Young Martin Genge (on tenor sax) was already known to some of the band from tours they had made with him in Ralph Laing's Groove Juice Special, while Nick Cooper was a natural to replace Ray on clarinet and alto sax. Both were agreeable and there was a warm and fond farewell to Ray and Janice at Yesterdays where the new additions played at their first session with the band. Chris Pope had meanwhile agreed to manage the band and subsequently formed his own professional music agency, 'Live Music UK'.

So suddenly there were two new members in a band which for many years had relied upon 'head' arrangements (no music on the stand). The arrangements had been memorised from rehearsal. Intros, codas and breaks, once learnt were taken for granted. Fortunately both the newcomers were sight readers, i.e. could read music first time through, a rare talent within in the jazz ranks, even today. Music stands appeared, Geoff began writing out manuscript versions of the old favourites for the newcomers, and soon discovered that new arrangements could be more quickly and permanently introduced by means of written out arrangements than by the old method of aural trial and error. This is now standard procedure within the whole band - they have discovered the world of 'written down' music, while hopefully maintaining the spontaneity of improvisation at the same time.

Yesterdays suffered a severe fire in the mid - 1980s.... and the Avon Cities band was inserted into the Old Duke repertory on every alternate Friday night. They survived the crisis over the future musical policy of the Newcastle Brewery (who own the Duke), in the early 90s and still remain there as a Friday night institution at the time of writing.

The 'new' Avon Cities at Yesterdays in 1983. From L to R: Mike Hitchings, trombone; Martin Genge, tenor sax; Frank Feeney, guitar; Geoff Nichols, trumpet; Chris Pope, drums; Dave Collett, piano; Nick Cooper, clarinet, and Clive Morton bass.

There have been further changes in the line- up in recent years. John Barton on alto/clarinet has become the main regular of a pool of reading reed players who can easily fit into place according to the band's requirements. Nick Cooper still guests with the band, while Martin and Frank Fennell share the tenor/clarinet spot.

Tony Baylis joined the band in 1989 and has since left us to live and work in Spain. John Morton has replaced him, while Frank Feeney has given way to Andrew Barratt from Bridgwater (though he needed to buy a banjo for use in the traditional numbers, which the band still play).

In 1989, the Avon Cities celebrated its fortieth anniversary with a concert at the Theatre Royal, from which two cassettes were subsequently issued. The concert covered nearly all the Avon's musical history (even the Skiffle was represented by Dave singing "How Long?" with Mike on mandolin and Geoff on bass, playing those instruments for the first time in twenty five years).

The band's fiftieth anniversary, in 1999, began with a celebratory concert at the Q.E.H.Theatre in January. A Jubilee C D, "Tempo Fugit",was issued, ("a real beauty" wrote Ken Rattenbury in the Jazz Rag). There was also a cruise to New York on the QE2, the band receiving standing ovations at their evening concerts in the Grand Lounge, plus an appearance at the Red Blazer Jazz Club in Manhattan and flying back to play their own jubilee concert at the Theatre Royal. Ray bush flew over from California to be with his old buddies, and the programme reflected the long and glorious history of Bristol's Jazz Jewell in the Crown.

Information supplied by Avon Cities
Editor

THE BLUE STAR QUINTET

The Blue Star Quintet had its genesis in 1947. Jack Toogood, recently demobilised from the Army teamed up with Les Drake whom he had known since schooldays. Les Drake, who played piano had also been in the army and having survived Dunkirk went on to accompany Jessie Matthews (film star, dancer and singer) when she entertained the troops. Les in the late 1930s had played piano in a group that had backed Coleman Hawkins who toured the U K promoting the Selmer tenor Sax for the Selmer Music Company.

Les introduced Jack to Don Burnell who had recently returned to Bristol after serving in the RAF. Don played tenor sax and clarinet, and with the recruitment of drummer Sid

Les Drake on piano and Jack Toogood on guitar, two of the founder members of the Quintet. Photo taken at a private function in July 1986.

Barnes and Norman Cole on bass the Blue Star Quintet was ready for their first gig in the Bristol area. There then followed a period of regular gigs at Shirehampton, but a regular spot was not easy to find.

Sometimes the band would have an extra musician in the form of Ron Ashen, who was a multi-instrumentalist and played jazz accordion. He also played the vibes and saxophone; this gave the band more voices and an extra dimension. With the extra member of the band they became the Blue Star Sextet.

In the early 1950s there was a breakthrough for the Blue Star Sextet when they were given a chance to broadcast from

Bristol on the West Home Service of the BBC. Duncan Wood was the producer. Many readers will remember him, although not so many will know that he played jazz trumpet, and is mentioned as playing at the Bristol Jazz Club in the late 1940s and early 50s.

This first broadcast led to other BBC engagements, with broadcasts from the Bristol studios. Mac McCoombe, a violin player from London, playing in the Joe Venuti style, joined the Quintet. In a broadcast in 1951 from the Whiteladies Road Studios of the BBC. Steve Race was the compere for the programme 'Jazz Interlude'. The band, now for a while the Mac McCoombe Quintet played "We Couldn't Say Goodbye", "After You've Gone", "Old Man Harlem" and "My Honey's Loving Arms."

Between the 1950s and 1970s the Blue Star Quintet or Sextet continued to broadcast on an occasional basis and played regular gigs, although not having a regular residency. They continued to play into the 1980s but the untimely and much lamented death of Les Drake in 1987 brought to an end the Quintet's swinging sound. In 1999 Don Burnell, the other founder member died, bringing to an end fifty years of music making in the Goodman/Hot Club swinging style. Looking back and reminiscing about musicians he had played with, Jack remarked that there was only one Les Drake.

Editor's interview with Jack Toogood

Don Burnell, another founder member playing at a private function in July 1986.

THE 1950s

ATLANTA JAZZ BAND

The band started in the 1950s in the unlikely setting of Kingswood Park, near Bristol. They played weekly in the open air for ballroom dancing. Starting as a duo called the 2Ds the band appeared with the introduction of other musicians including Cliff Burnham, banjo; and Brian Huggett, sax, now a member of the Severn Jazzmen.

Between 1950 - 1960 they were known as the Jubilars Jazz Band, a strict tempo group. The rhythm section broke away and were joined by trumpeter Bill Grieves, whose interest was in the trad idiom. This line-up became the Atlanta Jazz Band. Other members of the band were Pete Hull, trombone; Clive Taylor, clarinet; Cliff Burnham, banjo; Keith Arnold, piano and Ron Morgan, drums. This line up lasted until 1970.

The bands first rehearsals were in an upstairs room of the Earl Russell, Lawrence Hill. While the customers drank in the bar below Bill and the boys spent a couple of months belting out the old favourites, providing free entertainment for the clientele.

The Atlanta Jazz Band soon acquired a weekly booking at the Grove Hall, Fishponds. By 1963 they were playing at the Crown and Dove, Bridewell, another weekly booking. It was during this period that the band was complemented by George Foster Flett, who played the E flat sousaphone and the tuba. George rated a column in the Bristol Evening Post in June 1963, the fact that he made a round trip of 200 miles to play at the Crown and Dove being considered newsworthy.

Alan Dracup, the pub manager, was heard to say "George is

incredible, he bundles his sousaphone into his mini every week and drives from Portsmouth, plays a three hour session and then drives all the way home again".

The style of the band was strictly New Orleans.

A change of line-up occurred during this time, Clive Taylor being replaced by Derek Joynson.

In 1970 the band changed it's name for the last time to the Atlanta Show Band, with vocalist Shirley May joining the line-up.The band ceased playing in early 1972.

Compiled from information from members of the Atlanta Jazz Band
Editors

BLUE NOTE JAZZ BAND

1956....... STILL GOING ....

One day in the late fifties, a group of young jazz musicians called on Ron Wallington, landlord of the Ship Inn in Redcliff Hill, Bristol. They asked if he'd let them hire his upstairs club room. Ron rang the local police station at Bedminster for advice. "I don't like it, Mr Wallington," said superintendent Whalley. "I don't like it at all".

But Ron decided to risk it. They were , as he said later, "a decent type of kiddie", and The Blue Note Jazz Club began. Supt. Whalley stationed a constable outside every Wednesday night for the first few weeks, until it became apparent that civil disorder was not about to break out. The constable vanished, only to reappear about six months later, climbing the stairs with measured tread to the consternation of Mike Welch on the door. "Mr Welch" he inquired."Yes". "Er....Might I join?" asked the P C.

There was in fact, one police raid. Nothing to do with drink, fighting or drugs,[DRUGS?... we wouldn't know one if we saw one]. No, the raid was about dancing. The Old Ship had a somewhat dodgy floor, and the jivers were a touch energetic. Also they tended to let in rather more people than the licence allowed, so there were real fears that dancers, listeners and band were on the point of cascading down into the bars below - so they stopped the dancing, that is until the police went away.....

It was at the Ship that I found the Blue Notes. Dispatched home from West Kirby by the RAF because of my feet, I resumed life as an Evening Post reporter, only to be exiled again, this time to Stroud by an editor who decided if the Air Force wasn't going to toughen me up, then he was. Because I couldn't drive a car I was issued with a black Vespa on which I wobbled around the Cotswolds, and eventually, one night, back to Bristol in search of bright lights, civilisation and culture.

After a year of evenings dominated by Minchinhampton Parish Council and Nailsworth Amateur Dramatic Society, the upstairs room at the Ship was like heaven.

The band played on a small stage in front of faded gold curtains at one end of the room: the bar was under a rickety balcony at the other. The Blue Notes at the time had a conventional line - up, but already there had been a number of changes. Trumpet players Mike Cocks and Chris Rice, trombonist Phil Fox and bassist [Chaffer] Knowles for instance had left: the stalwarts were now John Hooper at the piano, Paul Hawkins on trombone, John Viner on banjo, Mike Long on bass, and the two Daves, Kingston and Jackson on trumpet and drums.

Unfortunately the clarinettist Al Morgan became ill and had to stop playing. His misfortune was my lucky break. I became a Blue Note flogging my way down from Stroud on the vespa with a clarinet strapped to the carrying rack. Often the landlord Ron had a bucket of hot water ready for me to thaw out my fingers.

The Blue Notes appearing before a lively audience at the Ship Inn, Redcliffe, 1960s.

Then we had a bit of a shake-up which accidentally created what's become the Blue Note sound. We lost our trumpet player, and David Challis turned up in Bristol to work on the newspaper, bringing his clarinet. Sickeningly, he was better than me, so to stay in the band I offered to lead on soprano sax for a while, until we found a trumpet player. [Crusty] Martin and Geoff Hancock joined on drums and bass, Crusty at that time carrying his entire kit around in a bubble car, out of which the drums would literally roll when he opened the door.

The new line-up gave us the chance to try a wider range of jazz than just the old standards: and John Hooper and Dave Challis led the campaign for regular rehearsals and original material. As a result we got noticed, and found ourselves playing, for instance, at the Berlin Philharmonic, in Zurich and Hanover, and at the Richmond Jazz and Blues Festival at which we were billed above the Rolling Stones.["They'll never catch on", we muttered as they pouted and twanged away in the marquee.]

Manager Mike could stand the excitement no longer and went to Australia, to be replaced by Keith Yates. Dave went to the BBC and Paul to sell foreign stamps in London: in came Nic Cooper and Mike Whitehead.

The fame of The Ship spread: at one time, the Alex Welch

17

band came down for regular guest sessions at £40 a time. No, not per man, for the whole band!

Our famous Christmas parties included a compulsory performance of 'submarines'- a Bentine like portrayal of the war in the Atlantic with Crusty and Geoff on periscopes. One year the band cabaret included a parody of the Magic Roundabout with Crusty as Dougal, Johnny Hoops as Brian the snail and me as Florence. I bet Duke Ellington never did anything like

The band at a 1964 gig in Bath. Musicians in view: Dave Challis, clarinet; Roger Bennett, soprano sax; Paul Hawkins, trombone, and John Viner, banjo.

that. Then...disaster. The planners decided to demolish the Ship and the historic Shot Tower next door for road widening. Well, it was either us or St Mary Redcliffe church. They did that sort of thing in 1968. We had an emotional and very alcoholic last session, and Johnny tore out the piano keys and threw them to the crowd. This was not appreciated by the breweries Head of pianos who arrived the following week to collect the remains.

We wandered in the wilderness for a while, playing to the indifferent punters at the Golden Cue Billiard Club, and at Acker's old Crown and Dove until the bulldozers moved in there too. We seemed to give pubs the kiss of death, so it was

mildly surprising that Kon and Alma eventually said we could move to the Old Duke.

Later John Stone arrived with his trumpet from the Royal Marines, not to play, except on special occasions, but to run the pub. The Bog End flourished, and we played our part in making the Duke a Jazz Centre of 'World Renown'. There can't be many city pubs which are packed out on a Monday night.

The band continued to change, but apart from a spell with Norman Hill on trumpet, kept it's distinctive sound with the soprano lead. Ralph Laing came in as a forceful pianist and arranger, Johnny Skuse to play trombone and sing. Wayne Chandler, whom I'd known since we were five came back from the London scene to join us on banjo and guitar. We did radio and T V, went to Germany again, and to Malta for a beer festival which featured only one sort of beer.

One episode, which sadly came to an end when the money ran out, was a series of concerts at, of all places, the Failand Hall, featuring jazz greats from America. Ruby Braff, Buddy Tate, Wild Bill Davidson, Peanuts Hucko, Ralph Sutton and Soprano Summit..... they all found themselves on a village hall stage performing to wild applause in front of scenery for the local pantomime.

Off went Ralph and Skuse to form Groove Juice. In came Chris Pearce on clarinet, Les Drake on piano and Tony Osborne on trombone. Tony had gone to London to teach, returned after twenty years, walked into the Duke and was greeted by, "Hello Tone, haven't seen you in the past few weeks..."

The Blue Notes stayed at the Duke for more than twenty years, making forays to agricultural shows, stately homes, weddings and funerals [we did Lord Bath's at Longleat and got our pictures in Hello Magazine]. We became resident band at Clevedon Jazz Club and played regularly at festivals there and at other seaside towns, Bude, Lyme Regis and Weymouth.

The Old Duke, King Street, 1996, with all the trimmings. Back Row: Chris Pearce, clarinet; Geoff Hancock, bass; Hannah Wedlock, vocals; Geoff Roberts, piano; Dave Hibberd, drums, and Tony Osborne, trombone. Front Row: on his own, Roger Bennett.

Redcliffe, within 100 yards of the old Ship Inn.

The band meanwhile is still going strong, Geoff Hancock and I are still there, despite doing day jobs which necessitate getting up around 4am. Young Chris Pearce on clarinet has become one of the old stagers: so is Geoff [Korg] Roberts who came in on piano after the tragic death of Les Drake.

Dave Hibberd, who was an occasional Blue Note in the past, returned to replace John Watson, a virtuoso player whose life suddenly took him to Milton Keynes. Ron Brown, who'd also been with us before, came back to replace Tony Osborne on trombone, the latter deciding after loyal service to study for yet another university degree. And, a special treat, a flower among the gnarled old jazzers, we added Hannah Wedlock. Her mum had persuaded us to let her sing "Summertime" at the Duke one night when she was only sixteen. We told her to go away and live a bit, which she was going to do anyway. Now she's back delighting audiences with her versions of songs from Bessie to Ella.

Every summer, come sun, rain or tempest, we took to the high seas, and sometimes very high seas, of the Bristol Channel for Riverboat Shuffles aboard the veteran ships Balmoral and Waverley. There was one memorable night in Portishead, when the band had to unload a piano in sheeting rain and pitch darkness; then carry it over swaying lock gates to the opposite quayside.

All good things, had to I suppose, have to come to an end, and our residency at the Old Duke finished abruptly after a bit of a tiff with the new management. We moved briefly to Bedminster and then to another quayside pub, The Pump House, before returning in the new millennium to the place where we started - Redcliffe. The Blue Note Jazz Club opened in March 2000 in the Undercroft of St. Mary

The Blue Notes, second only to the Avons in endurance, are due to celebrate their 50th birthday in the year 2006.

We are planning to stick around for the party.

Roger Bennett

CASSEY BOTTOM

The origins of the Cassey Bottom band start with childhood friendships. Reg Quantrill and Keith Box would mime to the recordings of Sid Phillips using toasting fork and poker as make believe guitar and clarinet instruments. Their enthusiasm eventually led to acquiring real instruments and involving some of their more musical friends in their music making. Terry Fry was encouraged to buy a trombone. Reg recalls seeing this instrument newly purchased and how impressed they all were. Ron Ford got a bass and they rehearsed in Roy Smith's mother's home in the lane that gave the band its name, Cassey Bottom.

Roy Smith was doing National Service and was a drummer in the forces; he rehearsed with the rest of the band when home on leave. The bands line-up about 1953 was Keith Box, clarinet; Geoff Allen, trumpet; Terry Fry, trombone; Ron Ford, bass; Roy Smith, drums, and Reg Quantrill on banjo.

One of the band's first gigs was at the old Y M C A tennis court pavilion, Great George Street, where the Avon Cities had their club. Reg recalls the band doing a very extended version of "Shall I walk through the streets of the city."

Cassey Bottom made two records in 1953 on the Graph records label, produced by Stan Strickland of Denmark Street. About this time Geoff Allen left to join the army and Reg moved to London, as did several other jazz musicians at this time. While there he played with the Crane River band, the Storyville band and Mike Peter's band.

Reg retuned to Bristol and between 1960 and 1963 played with the Stainer/Collett 7 band. He re-formed the Cassey Bottom band, the nucleus of which was Keith Box, Terry Fry and Roy Smith. By 1963 they had a residency at the Crown and Dove in Bridewell on Saturday nights, and during this period they had several trumpet players from London, Tony Larkins, Trevor Williams, Mike Peters and Mike Tyzak.

Other musicians who have played with Cassey Bottom include Roy Reed, trumpet; John Macey, John Phipps and (Bas)Dark, bass, and Les Solomons, trumpet and trombone.

A 1950s photo of Cassey Bottom on a flat bed lorry. Standing: Keith Box, clarinet. Seated L to R: Hidden behind a tuba is, allegedly, Brian Walker, Terry Fry, trombone; Reg Quantrill, banjo and Roy Smith, drums.

When famous bands on tour visited the city they would some times drop in after their performance, and Reg recalls members of Eddie Condon's Band 'sitting in' and on another occasion some of George Lewis's Band joined the Cassey Bottom for an impromptu but very enjoyable session.

During 1964/65 Reg was with Mike Cocks' New Chicagoans and then followed nine years with the Wurzels. Since then Reg has fronted the Reg Quantrill Quintet with Bob Wade,

Reg Quantrill's later band, the Gentlemen of Jazz at a gig at Dillington House, Somerset 1980s. Back Row L to R: Reg Quantrill, guitar; Bobby Mickleburgh, trombone; Alan Taylor, bass, and Al Walker, tenor sax. Seated: the late Alan Scott.

trumpet; John Hopkins, trombone; Alan Taylor, clarinet, and the other Alan Taylor on bass. The Gentlemen of Jazz is Reg's most recent band; the line up a few years ago was Al Walker, reeds; Alan Scott, trumpet; Bobby Micklelburgh, trombone, and Alan Taylor, bass.

Cassey Bottom and the Public Services.
Very few musicians had cars in the 1950s and so bands got to and from gigs by public transport or walked. Late one night, Reg, Keith and Roy were carrying their instruments home from central Bristol when they were stopped by the police and questioned. Eventually the law were convinced they had not nicked the instruments and Reg asked if they would mind giving them a lift home, which they nobly agreed to, this included getting Roy's drums in the police car. When Roy was dropped off at Troopers Hill Keith and Roy didn't get

out, "We live in Cadbury Heath", they said, and after a few moments of deep thought the law took them all the way. This meant crossing the border from Bristol to Gloucestershire, serious stuff in those days.

The Cassey Bottom had a New Years gig at the Crown and Dove which was unusually poorly attended. There was a big party going on in the Fire Station across the road. Someone suggested that the two groups amalgamate and a very good time was had by all. The bonus for the band was an early morning lift home in a fire engine!

Editor's interview with Reg Quantrill

CHEW VALLEY JAZZ BAND

RUSTIC RE-BIRTH OF THE BLUES
Recollections of the Chew Valley Jazz Band 1950-1993

My personal recollections of the birth pangs and subsequent renaissance of jazz in this corner of the West Country began appropriately enough, according to my diaries, at a Labour Party meeting in the Village Hall at Stanton Drew on the 28th of November, 1950, at which the socialist candidate, a Mrs Xenia Field, was to attempt, unsuccessfully as it transpired, to drum up enthusiasm for her cause to a farming and coal-mining audience. A little light relief to all the political fire and emotional brimstone was the appearance of four young men, who played four numbers ("Sister Kate", "Dark Town Strutters Ball", "The Saints" and "Snag it!") before the interval, then, refreshed by tea and home made cakes, into which

Chew Valley Jazz Band at the Old Schoolroom, Chew Magna, on the 31st May 1952. L to R: Roy King (Onk), banjo; Q Williams, piano; Acker Bilk, clarinet; Cliff Brown, drums; John Hill, cornet; Mike Redston, bass; Brian Walker, tuba, and John Skuse, trombone.

they made ravenous inroads, returned to the stage to play the same four tunes, with one noticeable variation - a quite sophisticated coda at the end of their performance. Half a century later I was to learn that one instrumentalist was so overcome by nerves that he failed to stop, and the coda was the result of his comrades rallying round in a demonstration of loyal and ingeniously gifted improvisation, a manoeuvre typical of jazz, and which subsequently I was to witness and take part in many times in the future. An introduction to 100% pure, unadulterated sterling jazz. The instrumentalists were John Skuse (trombone), Keith Parsons (piano), Roy King (trumpet) and Bernard Bilk (clarinet and leader).

My diary doesn't record the reactions of the audience (though, as I've indicated, Mrs Field lost the election, regretfully), but I was captivated. From being a narrow-minded upholder of orchestral and chamber music (mind you, we would have been inundated by performers of the Donald Peers/By a Babbling Brook genre, at the time) I promptly sensed that what I had heard had echoes of the diet that had crackled out of the Cossor wireless of my 20s/30s childhood, and I pro-ceeded to broaden my horizons accordingly..........to the extent of staging the first ever Labour Party Jazz Band Ball at the conservative and unadventurous village of Chew Magna, on the 26th of March, 1951, and played by that most notable of provincial bands, the Avon Cities Jazz Band. It was a huge success, and here I renewed acquaintance with my four Stanton Drew performers, who had come along to listen, and I accepted an invitation to come to a practice blow at the Miners' Welfare Hall at Pensford.

Now, to preclude too much repetition, I will revert mainly to some notable dates and comments from my diaries - many incidental dates being omitted..........

11th April 1951: Listen to a practice at Pensford - Skuse being drilled in his "Snake Rag" solo by Acker (erstwhile Bernard Bilk) pushing the trombone slide into its various required positions and requested to "hit that (Anglo-Saxonism deleted) note, 'Skid'!"

5th May: Practice at Pensford - am let loose on the drums; am informed that I'm "useless but have a steady beat", (an opinion which has continued with some justification, throughout my subsequent jazz career).

22nd September 1951: First recorded 'gig' - at the Drill Hall, Old Market. Bumptious R.S.M. queried the number of our personnel (Secretary, myself; Manager, Zank - an old school fellow of Acker's, and three girls - Essential Psychological Support Team. Oppressive atmosphere. First diary mention of G.Q. Williams (piano) and Cliff Brown (Drums) and Glyn Wilcox (trumpet), Tiger Yates was on banjo. The bass was a five gallon oil drum surmounted by a teak stem and a grandfather clock catgut weight cord for a string, all plucked and thumped with great enthusiasm by an old school-fellow of mine, Mike Redston.

20th October 1951: Another gig at the Drill Hall. Myself on drums (see above for my possible contribution) - Cliff Brown unable to play on this occasion; banjo now taken over by the regally named Royston Reginald King (popularly known as "Onk" - another school fellow of Acker's) and on trumpet was John Stainer. Our manager was the memorable T.K. Daniels.

14th December 1951: Played at the Avon Cities Club at Great George Street.

15th December: Played at Filton Memorial Hall.

January 1952: Band practices now at The Old Schoolroom, Chew Magna. The band has been told to vacate the Miners' Welfare Hall at Pensford, as the noise was putting the billiard players off their game. Typically, Acker had told them we were going to leave anyway, as the sound of their balls knocking together put the band off its music.

January 1952: Now followed the formation of the final Chew Valley Jazz Band (of great memory). On 1st March 1952 John Hill replaced John Stainer, playing a delightful driving round-toned cornet. I, who had been learning to find my way round a baritone horn which had belonged to Onk's father (ex-Pensford Prize Silver Band) expended the whole of the band's financial capital (£5) on buying an E flat (Eb) Besson tuba at Bristol Band Instrument Co. at Lawrence Hill (blessings on the memory of old Mr Iles). I was ruthlessly taught to play it, after a fashion, by Acker. He moulded and bullied us into shape, taught us to LISTEN, and operate as a BAND, and, under his tuition, encouragement and leadership we developed, for an amateur village band, an individual tone and quite a respectable repertoire - such numbers as "What d'you call 'em Blues", "Milenburg Joys", "Melancholy Blues", "Willy the Weeper" and an absolute peach of an original Bilk tune, "Old Schoolroom".

Throughout 1952 the C.V.J.B flourished, playing gigs at Whiteladies Ballroom, our own club at the Old Schoolroom (we had a couple of packed Jazz Band Ball sessions there), RAF South Cerney and a momentous Riverboat Shuffle. We now practised in an old shed and an antique bus-body in Onk's back garden. We even tried a Bristol club, Club Creole in St Michael's Hall - unsuccessfully, the last venture. The band played it's last gig at a Jazz Band Ball at the Church Hall, Chew Magna on 6th December 1952.

It's last gig, LAST gig? Well, we had an intermission, probably one of the longest on record. Although we were all to meet up on different occasions in the meantime, it wasn't until the 28th February and 7th March 1993 - 41 years later - that we were all together again with instruments in our hands, when we made a tape we called "Odyssey" - an historically, if not musically, interesting and memorable performance. I am reminded that the lights failed during the musical interlude, and the pianist rendered "Alligator Crawl" while the caretaker, with the aid of a candle, replaced the fuse.

Brian Walker

IMPERIAL JAZZ BAND

The Imperial Jazz band was first formed in the mid 1950s in a scout hall at Combe Down, Bath. The original members of the band were Terry Emery, trumpet; Clive Holloway, clarinet; Pete Ward, or Ned Kelly, trombone; Chuck New, banjo; Norm Bishop, bass; or Robert (Crow) Coles, brass bass; (Whiskers) Williams, drums. The band was later joined by Glyn Wilcocks on piano who was also playing trombone with the Apex Jazz Band. The Apex Band consisted of: Glyn Wilcocks, Pearce Cadwallader, Ian (Flurge) Appleyard, Norm Bishop, Frank Feeney and Bart Carpenter.

This original Imperial Jazz Band ran the very successful Bath Jazz Club at the Angel Hotel, now called the Westgate, in Westgate Street, Bath, in the late fifties.

As well as playing locally the band ventured further afield and on Christmas 1958 played an all-nighter at the Ken Colyer club with the Colyer Band, The Alberts and the late Jim Lougher Band. Cy Laurie also guested with the band at the Angel. The band continued until about 1960.

On his return to England from Australia, in 1966, where he had been playing with The Melbourne New Orleans Wanderers, Nigel Hunt (who had previously played in Bath as a founder member of the Riverside Jazzmen and also the Pearce Cadwallader Stompers), decided to revive the name of the Imperial Jazz Band. The members of this band were Nigel Hunt, Trevor Bricker, Terry Fry, (Fingers) Davis, Den Morris and Pete Ward.

Of this original reformed line-up only Nigel Hunt and Pete Ward remain. Of the others, one became a Mormon Bishop, one jumped from the roof of a hospital, one disappeared to Germany and the other has not been seen since. Does this say something about the music?

The band played for John Bradshaw at the Bell, Bath, in the late 60s and early 70s. John still talks of the great after hours blow they had with the late Joe Harriet, and Pete Ward still

Nigel Hunt, leader of the Imperial Jazz Band on trumpet, with Mike Cooper on trombone.

24

remembers Mary's sandwiches, as well as having a regular Thursday and the Saturday night at the Duke, Bristol, with Con and then John Stone.

The band appeared on the first Old Duke compilation recording.

The band has had quite a number of changes over the last 25/30 years and during that time have had such musicians as: Dave Stone, Alan Scott, Nick Cooper, Derek Joynson and Gary Price, clarinet; Graham Freeman, Bob Reynolds, Bobby Mickleburgh and Warren Short, trombone; Jay Hawkins, John Gill and Richard (Woody) Wood, Banjo; Nick De'Fosard and Mike Lines, bass; Pete Winterhart, Roger Wells, drums.

The present line-up of the band has, apart from one or two changes, remained the same for the last three or four years and consists of: Nigel Hunt, trumpet; Neil Dunning, clarinet; Tom Whittingham, trombone; Pete Ward, bass; Malc Hurrell and Billy Scott, banjo; Colin Bushell, drums.

Of the band's style and policy Nigel Hunt says "Because the band is so compatable and sympathetic to each other I don't feel I am only speaking for myself when I say our style is in the New Orleans tradition. Although I, like the rest of the band, in the past have done our 'apprenticeship' with bands that play classic revival jazz, i.e. Morton, Oliver, Hot Fives and Sevens etc., I have always, with the Imperial Band, preferred to continue the tradition of the bands of the New Orleans dance halls, playing music of the time, music that is not dated or 'mouldy,' and music that is good to dance to. Although I enjoy and admire the musicians and music of the 20s and 30s, and also the second-generation musicians of New Orleans, I feel that one should not go backwards or stagnate but that jazz should be allowed to develop naturally. I believe this can be done and still remain within *the tradition*".

Recent recordings of the band are: IMPERIAL JAZZBAND "Purveyors of Music in the New Orleans Style". Recorded Bath 1996. Available as tape or CD.

IMPERIAL JAZZBAND "On a Coconut Island". Recorded live at the 1997 Bude Jazz Festival. Also one track used for festival compilation recording. Available as tape or CD.

Compiled from information supplied by Nigel Hunt
Editors

PARAMOUNT JAZZ BAND

1952-1957
ACKER AND THE FORMATIVE YEARS

I first heard Acker Bilk one Saturday afternoon in the Miners' Welfare Hall in Pensford. This was where the Chew Valley Jazz Band used to practice in the early 1950s. Acker worked out the chords on an old upright piano that languished in one corner and, as well as playing the clarinet he seemed to know instinctively the correct valve positions on the trumpet and slide positions on the trombone - even if their players did not! I was attempting to learn to play the trumpet, and played with this group on a few occasions until they found someone who could actually play the instrument. I went back to trying to develop my trumpet technique, and to picking tunes and phrases of classic jazz records as they became available.

At that time our principal influences were the 1920s recordings of King Oliver, Jelly Roll Morton, and the Louis Armstrong Hot Five and Hot Seven. The 1940s recordings by the Bunk Johnson and George Lewis Bands conveyed to me, and to many others, the authentic sound of the contemporary, live, jazz of New Orleans.

I never imagined that, some ten years on, George Lewis himself would travel all the way from New Orleans to London to appear on a TV show - "Acker Bilk - This is your life".

The Paramount Band at the Crown and Dove. Musicians, L to R: Chick Hatch, bass; Acker Bilk, clarinet; Roy (Onk) King, guitar; John Stainer, trumpet; Michel Worms (french), banjo; Kloop Cox, drums and Dave Collett, piano. Among the dancers are Mark Cottell, Dudley Felix, Pete Harrison and the actor Peter O'Toole.

In 1952 we formed a little band with a front line of trumpet and two clarinets. The clarinettists were Pete Conibear and Acker Bilk, with me on trumpet. Dave Collett joined us on piano and during these early days the rhythm section variously included a Frenchman, Michel Worms, on banjo, Roy King (a.k.a. "Onk") - guitar, Chick Hatch and Mark Cottell - bass, with John (Kloop) Cox and Mike Braund on drums. (Peter O'Toole appears as one of the dancers in a photo of an early club session).

The band needed a name, but what? Various options were discussed and rejected - none seemed sufficiently appropriate or inspirational. I browsed through the names on labels of old records - Genet, Okeh, Paramount.............that's it! Paramount! Lets call ourselves the PARAMOUNT JAZZ BAND. There was instant agreement and Acker has retained the name to this day.

The Paramount Jazz Band played once a month in the upstairs room of the Crown and Dove Hotel, just off the City Centre, and quickly established an enthusiastic following. Soon it was every Tuesday evening at the Crown and Dove and eventually we expanded to Saturdays as well. John Skuse joined on the trombone, and the rhythm section established itself as Dave Collett - piano, Jay Hawkins - banjo, Johnny Macey - bass, and Roy Smith - drums. For us, at this time, the top band on the national scene was Ken Colyers Jazzmen but, in October 1954, Chris Barber and Monty Sunshine parted company with Ken, taking the rhythm section with them. Ken started to form a new band and was looking for a clarinet player to match his exacting ideals. Pete Conibear went up to London to meet Colyer. They got on well but mutually agreed it would not be an ideal match. Pete advised Ken that he felt that the right clarinet player for Ken's new band would be - Acker Bilk.

Acker and Ken were a good match. Acker joined Ken Colyers Jazzmen and moved up to London. Having to start from scratch again meant going through a lean time for the new band. However they recorded an LP for Decca - "Back to the Delta" - and Acker's playing attracted attention on the London scene and further afield. It was an uphill struggle and, after nine months, Acker left and returned to Somerset. (In the meantime Pete Conibear had left Bristol and the Paramount Jazz Band was without a clarinet player).

The Bristol jazz scene was now transformed. The old band was re-invigorated and relaunched as ACKER BILK'S PARAMOUNT JAZZ BAND. There was now a band and club to rival the long established Avon Cities Jazz Band! We were an entirely co-operative band, with Acker as the leader, and me handling the telephoning and correspondence with agents. Lyn Dutton, who was agent for Humphrey Lyttelton, started to provide a regular series of weekend bookings around the London and Manchester clubs.

The next step was to get into records. Stan Strickland, of Stan's Record Shop, recorded five numbers for us in the basement of the Victoria Methodist Church, Clifton. Decca was not interested, but I got an encouraging response from Carlo Krahmer of Esquire Records. Carlo had the reputation for taking a commercial chance with up and coming bands and musicians, and bought our tape outright for £20! The band

The front line of the Paramount Jazz Band at the Crown and Dove in 1956. L to R: John Stainer, Acker Bilk and John Skuse.

members were elated! We were on record at last. Initially two 78s were released - "My Old Kentucky Home/Gravier Street Blues", and "Gettysburg March/Over in Gloryland". Later, Esquire re-issued all four tracks on a 45 rpm EP as "Master Acker Bilk".

The Jazz Club at the Crown and Dove now featured, from time to time, guest artists with the band. I recall Ken Colyer, George Melly, and Bruce Turner, among others. In addition to being a world-class alto sax player, Bruce Turner was also a well-known eccentric. So, when he said to me - "I'm getting a band together to play in Poland, will you and Roy come with me, Dad?", Roy Smith and I thought this a rather eccentric form of humour. But he meant it. The Bruce Turner

Quintet, that subsequently played several performances in Warsaw, including recording for a Polish record company, comprised Bruce (alto and clarinet), Johnny Parker (piano), Jim Bray (bass) with me on trumpet and Roy Smith on drums. This was also the start of a romance, as Roy met Krystyna in Warsaw (but I must not digress).

In a conversation with someone from Polish Radio, I had mentioned Acker and our band from Bristol. Some months

John Stainer on trumpet, during a performance with Acker Bilk's Paramount Jazz Band, 1956, Bristol.

later this chap, Maciek, contacted me to say that he would be visiting London and would like to hear the Paramount Jazz Band if we were playing somewhere nearby during the time of his visit. By a stroke of luck we were booked along with the bands of Terry Lightfoot and Dave Cary to play the "Jazz Scene 56"concert at the Royal Festival Hall. (This concert was recorded by Decca and we had three tracks in the "Jazz Scene 56" LP - "Really the Blues", "Where the River Shannon Flows", and "Dippermouth Blues"). "Why don't you come along and meet us all at the Royal Festival Hall?". I suggested.

Maciek was suitably impressed, and we subsequently succeeded in negotiating with a Polish Government department for a two-week concert tour in late September/early October of that year.

Shortly before departure for Poland we were faced with a dilemma. John Skuse left and we were faced, at very short notice with finding a replacement trombonist. We were fortunate in finding Alan Rodely - a keen young university student. There was hardly time to rehearse the new front line before setting off on tour but Alan, with his youthful good looks was a wow with the Polish fans.

The tour package comprised a Polish Quintet who played the first half of each concert, and our band who came on for the second half. Jeanne Johnstone, an ex-patriate Englishwoman living in Warsaw was added as vocalist with the Paramount Jazz Band. With no time for rehearsal we sorted out some numbers with Jeanne, and agreed keys and simple head arrangements on the coach as we were rushed to our first show - at Poland's second city, Lodz. Now it so happened that Lodz was the hometown of Krystyna, who Roy had met in Warsaw the year before. Krystyna was there to meet the band - this time she and Roy became engaged. (They were later married back in Bristol and brought up a family there - but again, I must not digress!).

The tour was a test of the band's stamina. We played 30 concerts in 10 towns and cities - every performance a full house. The biggest audience was 8,000 people in the "Peoples Hall" in Wroclaw. After the final show in Warsaw we were taken to an all-night farewell party, where numerous bottles of vodka were consumed in toasts to all and sundry. Somehow we all survived, and staggered onto the plane the following morning for our return home.

Back in Bristol the band made a broadcast, and Acker and I were interviewed on a BBC news programme. Acker was asked how the Polish audiences reacted to our music. "They went BERESK," replied Acker, adding to the English language a word that is now in common use among Bristol jazz

28

fans as they 'reminisce' about the good old days.

Success brought to a close the first chapter in the story of the Paramount Jazz Band. It gave Acker the experience and confidence to decide to launch into a fully professional career. The rest, as they say, is history.

John Stainer

PIONEER JAZZMEN

Jazz at the Cellar.

The Pioneer Jazzmen played in the cellar of the Communist Club in Lawfords Gate. The band started around 1961. Some of the personnel were as follows: Trevor Bricker, reeds; Fred Manners, piano; Dave Creech, trumpet; Pete Childs, trombone; John Hallier, drums; John Macey, bass, and Jay Hawkins, banjo. The late Paul Garland, the well known City politician was active in the club at this time, and later on became an active member of the Musicians Union.

The 60s was a decade of protest, (there was much to protest about) and the Pioneer Jazzmen were much sought after to be the vanguard of the many gatherings that took place in the city at that time. Supporters of Anti - Apartheid, Human Rights, C.N.D. and Trades Union activities were often cheered by the band's presence. They also took part in less serious events such as carnivals and University Rag parades.

The Club was a late night venue, starting after the pubs closed. Many members came over from the Crown and Dove and this ensured a lively and exuberant audience. Some club members to this day cannot remember how the club overcame the strict licensing laws of that time. On reflection, they feel the club survived on a mixture of careful planning and good fortune. However, by the mid 1960s the band had ceased to exist. There were probably many reasons for the club's demise, one could have been that some of the more politically minded members moved into the folk scene.

The Pioneer Jazzmen were musically in the New Orleans tradition with a strong adherence to the George Lewis style. Unfortunately there are no known recordings of this once exciting band.

Editor's interview with Dave Creech

The Pioneer Band on the march. This early 1960s photo was taken near Park Street. L to R: Trevor Bricker, clarinet; Gary Price, tenor sax; Fred Manners, drum; Dave Creech & Paul Gribble, trumpets. Standing behind Fred Manners is the late Paul Garland.

STAINER/COLLETT 7

John Stainer was never one to toe the party line. He was supposed to have scaled the topmost pinnacle of Clifton Suspension Bridge to paint left-wing slogans. He certainly organised the Paramount Band's Polish Tour behind the Iron Curtain in 1956. So when he formed a band in 1958, to play mainstream jazz, it was smack in the middle of the Trad boom.

He played trumpet and I played piano. Nick Cooper played the clarinet and tenor sax, which was a risky business then. Terry Fry played trombone, Sandy Miller, bass and Roy Smith, drums. Reg Quantrill played guitar and not banjo, which was derigeur at that time. Incredible as it may seem now the guitar and, more so the saxophone, inflamed passions to such a pitch that a petition was once 'got up' to have them banned. It didn't work.

The band played every Tuesday at the Ship on Redcliffe Hill, which has since been flattened and built upon. Later it also played Saturdays at the Bathurst Hotel, which is still standing, although now known as The Louisiana. Audiences were seldom enormous, but viable, and many people look back with affection to those times. Reg Quantrill, who 'knew someone' outfitted the band with uniforms; light grey jackets, black trousers, black socks and ties - £4.00 a set or £28.00 for the whole band! We looked sharp enough at a distance. For some reason all the jackets were the same length. Sandy Miller, who was twenty years older than the rest of us (or twenty years younger than we are now), was also a lot shorter. His coat hung low in the manner of a 'Prince Albert', favoured by Mississippi gamblers about the time Fort Sumpter was being fired upon. He was a veteran of the Grand Spa in the days of Fishy Williams (George Shearing had played there then - now it's called the Avon Gorge Hotel).

Sandy was addicted to snuff and had an unquenchable thirst.

During the early sixties something strange began to happen. Without warning an Inspector of Police accompanied by a Constable, would burst through the door. His ambition was to catch people dancing (men dancing with women that is). If this could be achieved he reckoned he could close the club down. This went on at jazz clubs all over Bristol.

At The Bathurst, where we played in an upper room, a warning light was installed in the ceiling. When the Inspector led the charge up the stairs, the Landlady pressed a button. By the time he reached the top everyone was seated. The Evening Post's correspondence columns were flooded with letters from outraged jazzers. The fact that other letters were appearing about 'proper mayhem' going unheeded in other parts of the city pointed up the farcical aspect of the dancing campaign. It all staggered to an unsatisfactory conclusion, but not before car-parking had somehow been linked with the prohibition of dancing.

One year, during the Season of Goodwill, John Stainer and his wife Jane applied for an extension at the Ship, so we could 'play in' the New Year. Naturally this was rejected. Jane pleaded with the Chief Constable, explaining how everyone would be disappointed. "I don't care Mrs STAMNER if its Tom Armstrong and his trumpet from London, you are not getting an extension"......not many bands have played in the New Year at 11.00pm!

Sometime in the early sixties, someone calling himself Uncle Bonney arrived in Bristol to cash in on the Trad boom. He opened something called The Chinese Jazz Club in the Corn Exchange. Despite it's daft name, Uncle Bonney was an occidental, and wore an occidental hat. True, it was made of straw, but more suited to the River Cam than the Yangstze. What's more he opened on Tuesday nights - our night. At about the same time The Blue Notes, who played the Ship on Wednesdays, won a jazz competition and appeared on TV - we hadn't entered, partly through snobbery and partly because the easiest thing to do in a competition is to lose.

The upstairs bar of the Ship Inn, Redcliffe Hill, with the Stainer/Collett 7 on their knees, possibly begging for a drink, but still looking happy. In this late 1950s photograph are, L to R: Dave Collett, Roy Smith, John Stainer, Nick Cooper, Reg Quantrill, Sandy Miller and Terry Fry.

As a result their audiences increased while ours dwindled. Uncle Bonney plastered his posters all over Bristol. We tore some of them down as a gesture, but we had no more chance than King Canute. This double blow marked the beginning of the end, and in 1963 we called it quits.

We must have been reasonably successful, since we were able to open twice a week - I can't recall other bands doing that. We broadcast and toured Cornwall, and generally had a good time. From time to time there were changes in the line-up, and these included Keith Box, Dr Derek Moore, Ron Brown and Chris Haskins. Keith was playing clarinet in the Artie Shaw style then, and joined on the condition that he wouldn't have to have a crew-cut like the rest of us. Dr Derek Moore was a lecturer in Mathematics and played clarinet.

Ron Brown had been recently demobbed from the RAF where he had played trombone in the station band. Consequently he had a blinding technique - the RAF don't stand no messing! Chris Haskins, who now plays in Switzerland, played bass. Strapped for cash on our Cornish tour he famously wrote home for money. I was present when he got back a Postal Order for 3/6d, which he converted into a pasty.

There were probably others whom I can't recall now - if so I apologise for their exclusion.

Adge Cutler often sat in and sang songs which would later make him a star when he formed The Wurzels. Reg also became a founder-member of Adge's band. T.K.Daniel would sometimes arrive in his tubular yellow overcoat and slouch hat. He would deliver his hilarious monologues, some of which have been preserved on tape. Most of the older jazzers can still do a creditable Ticky Daniel's impersonation.

Postscript.

Roy Smith doesn't play now and we lost touch with Derek Moore soon after the band broke up. Terry Fry, Sandy Miller, Ticky Daniel and Adge Cutler are sadly no longer with us. The rest of us still play regularly in various bands and with any luck should do so for a bit longer.

Dave Collett

THE 1960s

THE DAVE COLLETT TRIO

The trio as we know it today started it's chequered career in the town of Thornbury, playing every other Sunday evening in the lounge of the Black Horse. This was quite an event for the locals and the few regular jazz fans. These regular events took place in the middle to late 60s.

The alternative Sunday evenings had various pianists including Ron Griffin, Russ Morgan, John Chrichinson and Geoff Roberts. Neither memory nor research will reveal the names of the two other pianists who played there regularly

Quite a number of bass players were in residence with the trio during this period. They included: Spud Taylor who later turned professional, Bernie Attridge now a professional in the U.S.A. and the well-known and ubiquitous Geoff Weldrake.

The lounge of the Black Horse was not large, the place was crammed and people obviously liked what they heard on Sunday evenings. The Dave Collett Trio were doing their stint during a period when the whole country was being subjected to power cuts, which of course affects the amplification system. These cuts occurred so often that I suggested to Dave that he should write one of his now famous Blues about them. So he wrote a "Power Cut Blues" and whilst giving it a first and only performance the inevitable power cut happened! It was suggested that Dave had 'fixed' the cut in case he forgot the words.

The trio continued to the early 70s, surviving changes of landlords, but the end came when the pub revealed it had no full entertainment licence. No more Sunday evenings were possible.

In 1976 I was asked to provide some jazz at the Coach and Horses in St. Judes. I asked Dave to participate and the trio played the first two weeks, then Dave had other commitments and so I assembled a quartet which became known as the 'Don Burnell Quartet'

The next episode of the trio's 'journey into space'occurred a few years later in my then local pub, The Plough on Bedminster Down Road. I asked the manager Steve if he would give the Trio a go for a few Tuesdays and he readily agreed. The owner of the pub said he couldn't see how a trio could play Traditional Jazz. I told him he hadn't heard Dave Collett! Suffice to say we were there nine and a half years. When Dave was on holiday or had other gigs, dep' pianists included John Hooper, Geoff Roberts, Dave Small and Glyn Howells. From the start at The Plough our bass player was Geoff Miller, 'borrowed' from the 'Bath City Jazzmen', and other bands. He is still an integral part of the trio and rightly so.

November '93 was the trio's last performance at The Plough. After about three months a tip off from a friend led to another venue, The White Horse in West Street Bedminster. The first night, the 29th March '94 was truly memorable, there was no piano at the pub so the manager Dave Franklin 'found' one. It was 'in tune' but several semi-tones below concert pitch! How Dave and Geoff managed that evening I'll never know.

Originally the trio played every other Tuesday because it was thought by one of the Brewery's 'higher-ups' that if we played every week it would become stale. This arrangement only served to confuse the public, some of who turned up on the wrong week! So it came to pass that weekly sessions were allowed. Lots of new friends were made amidst the relaxed atmosphere of The White Horse and several new fans have become regular stalwarts.

Guest musicians were welcomed to 'sit in' with us, but this was, and still is, strictly limited, as too many guests quickly lose the identity of the band.

The year 1998 brought to fruition a project I considered to be long overdue. Dave Collett decided to put some of his numbers into book form and also recorded them on cassette. The book was published and recordings made of 15 of his songs and one of his instrumental numbers. The trio recorded the cassette at The White Horse one Sunday in August that year. At last this man's talent was on record and in print.

Dave Hibberd

The Trio at the White Horse, Bedminster. L to R: Dave Collett, piano; Dave Hibberd, drums, and Geoff Miller, bass.

THE EXCELSIOR JAZZ BAND

The band was originally formed in 1969 as the Mike Cooper Jazz Band to honour some gigs at the Granary, and carried on under that name until September 1973.The name Excelsior was adopted, not after the famed New Orleans Marching Band but after a band of the same name which hailed from Birmingham University which was led by the late Don Campbell. A good friend of mine, he was killed in a car accident in the 1960s. The band was named Excelsior in his honour.

Band members over the years have been: trombone, Mike Cooper; trumpets, John Keen, Norman Thatcher, Paul Keel, Bob Wade, Ian (Flurge) Appleyard, and Pete Martin; clarinets, Derek Joynson and Brian Huggett; bass, John Macey and Geoff Weldrake; piano, Rod Coleman until 1980 (no piano since); guitar/banjo, Wayne Chandler, John Viner, Brian Helliwell, Pete Barnard, Reg Quantrill and John Gill; drummers, Reg Harrison, Roger Wells, Crusty Martin, Frank Woodford and Brian Osborne.

The band, as the Excelsior Jazz Band, first

played at the Bristol Flyer in September 1973 and has subsequently had many regular residences at The Granary, The Old Duke, Crockers, Stonehouse, Pour House, Yesterdays, Mauretania, Bristol Bridge Inn, The Naval Volunteer, and others at Clevedon, Portishead and Weston-super-Mare.

I arrived one Thursday evening prior to playing at the Old Duke to find Campbell Burnap at the bar. He enquired whether it would be possible to 'sit in' with the band after he had finished playing on the Lightship recording for Ack's Half Hour. Our big bass player shouted "look out for board-

The bands line-up in 1982. From L to R: John Viner, guitar; Roger Wells holding the drum: Rod Coleman, piano; Geoff Weldrake, bass; John Smith, trumpet. Kneeling R: Derek Joynson, clarinet and seated, the leader, Mike Cooper on trombone

ers" as Campbell appeared on stage. Gradually, during the second half the rest of Acker's band joined in, including Johnny Parker on piano. John Stone, the landlord of the Old Duke at that time stopped the band to state that no sales would be possible after 11.pm.

We were playing in Taunton in the 1970s with Charlie Prince depping on trumpet. Charlie reckoned that he was half Red Indian, and arrived wearing a bandanna, sweatshirt and jeans. He was also sporting at the time an Afro-style haircut. The doorman, on seeing this apparition refused to let Charlie in. A discussion was rapidly called and the outcome was that he would still not be allowed in. The band's response was that if Charlie was not to be allowed in we would not be playing. Bearing in mind that we were due to start at 8.30 and the time was now 8.20 the management decided on a solution, this being that Charlie would be better suited in his appearance standing in the shadows at the back of the stage. Once again this was not acceptable to the band. The end of this saga was that Charlie played up front and became a 'wow' with the audience, who were mostly ladies of the older generation.

Mike Cooper

HENRY'S BOOTBLACKS

I was always a bit musical, attempting to play the piano from age two onwards. Formal piano lessons at age six were wasted; they stopped me from playing. I had my own way of doing things- often the wrong way- and to some extent this attitude has plagued me ever since. As soon as the lessons stopped, I started to play again. By ear I worked out simple melodies.

My father played the piano, in fact he composed, so there was music to be heard at home every day; one of my early memories is of sitting under the grand piano listening to Chopin Preludes.

In the mid fifties, although I didn't know it, jazz was all around me. Ted Heath and His Music were in the hit parade, The Ray Ellington Quartet and Max Geldray could be heard on the Goon Show (a great favourite of mine) and my aunt Louise had lots of Hot Dance '78' records which I would spin on the gramophone during the school holidays. While walking around I used to whistle improvised variations on the hit tunes of the day. When asked what I wanted "to do on leaving school", I said I thought I would become the leader of a dance band.

The definitive moment came when I saw the cover of the Radio Times for the first week of February 1957. Over evocative silhouettes of four young musicians (trumpet, clarinet, string bass and drums) the legend proclaimed a "Festival of Jazz"- imagine that now - some hope! The Royal Festival Hall was the venue for the Saturday night's live broadcast. We were treated to Kenny Baker's Dozen (nice!) and Cy Laurie and His Hot Seven, which later I, and a vociferous section of the audience, seemed to prefer. I was reminded that I'd heard something similar the previous New Year's Eve when I had caught a BBC West of England Home Service outside broadcast from a pub in Carhampton, near Minehead. The announcement "Acker Bilk and his Paramount Jazz Band" was followed by the most incredible 'row'- pure musical anarchy- I'd never heard anything like it. Cy Laurie was similar. I had to find out more!

My dad needed little encouragement in this direction and took me to some of the Sunday night jazz concerts at the Colston Hall in Bristol. Mick Mulligan, Cy Laurie and Chris Barber are those I remember. Barber's "Storyville Blues" was the second record I bought.

Dad and I went to a "Hi-fi" demonstration at the Grand Hotel in March 1957. Three young men, seated in the front row, showed signs of approval when a jazz record "Hawaiian War Chant" was played. When it finished they got up and left. I later realised that they were Ray Bush, Mike Hitchings and Geoff Nichols. That record was my first purchase.

Having discovered Stan's Record Centre, above Blake's Medical Store, No. 5, Denmark Street, Bristol, I purchased my third record. This was a new Vocalion '78' of Johnny Dodds & His Black Bottom Stompers. I'd heard Cy Laurie refer to Dodds so was keen to hear what he was all about. As soon as the first sounds came from the grooves I knew I had arrived at the Holy Grail!

At the time there were plenty of second hand '78s' about. I picked up King Olivers, Mortons as well as Armstrong Hot Sevens. Stan Strickland used to offer a service of copying deleted records from his collection onto your own customised acetates. A lot of my first Hot Fives came this way. They were soon worn out!

From the Bell Music Store in the Arcade came an old simple system clarinet. It looked like the one that Dodds is shown playing in the photos, but it didn't sound much like it when I played it. I learnt to play it by listening, and playing along with, records. In this I was in good company; the first jazz musician to do it was Bix Beiderbecke. My knowledge of the keyboard and chord structures helped in playing the clarinet and, in return, the playing of solo melodic lines on the clarinet expanded my approach to the piano.

I was in the fourth year at Chipping Sodbury Grammar School; our form room was the Physics Lab. At lunchtimes a group of sixth formers would troop through the lab. and disappear into the Preparation Room behind the blackboard. Intriguing musical sounds could be heard coming from this quarter. It turned out to be a clandestine jazz appreciation society. I offered to bring some records for them to hear, together with some critical notes, as a result of which they, somewhat reluctantly, let me join the 'club'.

One of these sixth formers was Alan Lishman who was friendly with John Lucena the elder brother of Gef who was in the year below me at school and was also learning the clarinet. I spent many happy hours at the Frenchay Friends Meeting House where they lived, listening to great jazz records. John is now running the Ratepayers Arms in Filton Community and Sports Centre and Gef Lucena is the well known record producer and owner of the specialist "Saydisc" label.

One Saturday afternoon in the spring of 1959 I heard a ten minute programme on the BBC Home Service featuring a newly released L.P. record of Johnny Dodds and Kid Ory. It was fantastic, I'd never heard any of the New Orleans Wanderers/Bootblacks or Chicago Footwarmers tracks before. I bought the record from Stan - it cost me nearly a whole week's wages. I met a young man at work who said that he wanted to play the tuba. As it happened I had just bought one, so I let him borrow it. He suggested that I try to play with a band that met in Boot Lane School, Bedminster, on Saturday afternoons, courtesy of the caretaker.

One Saturday in April 1960 I turned up with my clarinet. The trumpet player, Dave Fairman, didn't sound like a jazz player at all; very 'straight' and cloying. The clarinet player was loud but he just 'burbled', not in control rhythmically at all. That was Clive Taylor who went on to become a decent player. The rudimentary trombone was wielded by one Pete Hull who later had some success with the guitar, but more from his taxi business. Now we come to the 'rhythm section'; there was a chap called Pete (I forget his surname) who was nicknamed "The Monkey" because of an unfortunate resemblance to that creature when he played the banjo. He knew three chords, fair enough, but had no idea how to use them. He just played them one after the other, two bars each, in the same sequence (Tonic, Subdominant, Dominant and then Tonic again) regardless of the tune being played. The racket when this lot played the minor strain in "Willie the Weeper" had to be heard to be believed. The drummer, Miff, was always just that; 'miffed' because he was only ever seen to play a snare drum and cymbal- that was all the poor lad could manage on the 'bus! No bass player of course. I was able to add nothing to this ensemble with my clarinet.

After a while a 'new' trumpet player came along, Jed Collard,

who knew what a jazz trumpet should sound like. He also knew some good tunes, so to help the 'rhythm section' I tried out the school piano. Since I was playing the right chords I

The Bootblacks at the Ship, Redcliffe Hill on the 15th February 1965. Back Row L to R: Q Williams, the leader Henry Davies and Dick Farler. Front Row L to R: Brian Huggett, (Boots) Griffiths, Dave Emmett, Brian Mann, Jim Osborne, John Hallier and Terry Fry.

didn't 'fit in' and Mike Webb suggested that I seek out The Galleon Jazz Band which played on Tuesday evenings in the crypt of the Bridge Street Congregational Church, Barton Hill. I decided to pay a visit. This was a different thing altogether. The band was quite tidy.

Roger Jaques, the clarinet player, recognised me from one day when he and some of the others had seen me rush into Stan's Record Centre mumbling incomprehensibly and pro-

37

ceeded to the back where, standing up and still clad in my Harold Wilson type stiff Gannex mackintosh, I played the piano all hunched over and then rushed out again. The whole episode appeared to be a visitation from Henry Crun, one of the great Spike Milligan's creations fo the Goon Show. "Look lads," he said to the others when entered the crypt, "it's that Henry type!". He told me this later after we became friends. The name stuck, as nicknames do, and was adopted as a stage name very shortly afterwards. I was told that the Galleon band would soon be breaking up; Geoff Roberts, the piano player, was leaving so I filled in for a while until a re-formed band started rehearsing at the same venue on Wednesday nights. It never had an official name, being referred to as Farler's Rampant Nineteen, because cornet player Dick Farler was nineteen at the time. I recorded the band with my new 'semi-portable' Phillips tape recorder; I still have the tape.

The nucleus of the band, Dick Farler, Roger Jaques and myself, was expanded in 1961 when we advertised for new players. Two Bristol University students joined; Bob Phoenix on banjo and an engineer called Ivor Watts, whose trombone playing was such that he could have gone straight into a symphony orchestra! We revived the name Galleon Jazz Band. Jed Collard, who had been playing my Bb tuba, now joined us but a regular drummer with the right kit, and ability, never materialised.

We did a few little gigs, no regular 'club' residency at that stage. In February 1962 we entered the Bristol University Jazz Band Contest. We came fourth after a band from Plymouth. First and second were the Blue Note Jazzmen and the Pierce Cadwallader Stompers, with Pat Purchase singing.

In 1963 the famous Oriole Jazz Band finally disbanded, but Roy Reed (trumpet) and his brother-in-law, Brian Huggett tried to keep it going with the aid of two ex-Orioles, (Boots) Griffiths, banjo, and Graham Burbage, drums. I played piano and Dennis Danvers and Pete Hull played bass and trombone respectively. After an unsuccessful summer residency in a Weston-super-Mare pub, the band expired.
Working for Stan Strickland at his new shop, The House of

Sound in Marsh Street brought me into contact with many professional, as well as amateur, musicians as there was a recording studio at the back of the premises. One of the former was the bass player with the Denny Mann Orchestra at the Grand Spa Hotel (now the Avon Gorge). He let me have his spare double bass, for £30, and even gave me a free lesson.

I had always tried to get the band to play my 'arrangements'- little three horn 'heads' learned by heart, but in order to progress in this direction I had to become musically literate, something my father had tried to precipitate fifteen years before- remember the abortive piano lessons? I was helped in this by Rudi Blesh's "They All Played Ragtime". The first group of photographic plates in this book feature a miniature reproduction of the complete original John Stark edition of Joplin's "Maple Leaf Rag" and this I learnt, theme by theme. I had tried playing ragtime by ear from the LP re-issues of piano rolls but this find was marvellous, you just couldn't get ragtime sheet music in the Britain of 1962.

Clearly a new band had to be formed for me to practice the twin arts of bass playing and musical composition and arrangement. It had to play classic hot jazz of course. In December 1963, we started rehearsing at the Blue Boy pub (now the Gainsborough) in Lockleaze with Norman Thatcher, trumpet; Clive Taylor, clarinet; Terry Fry, trombone; 'Q' Williams, piano; (Boots) Griffiths, banjo; that is, three ex-Orioles, and John Hallier, drums. I had to play bass because I didn't know of a bass player who could play recognisable notes, let alone actually read music. At least, no-one who would lower themselves to play with me!

Two early personnel changes were Dave Emmett, trumpet, and Jim Osborne, clarinet, both good readers. They replaced Messrs Thatcher and Taylor, both of whom preferred playing less 'arranged' jazz. Six months and the band was ready to be let loose on an astonished Bristol public. The way this came about was interesting.

Roger Jaques had retired from the Galleon Band (to get married) in the autumn of 1962 and, in a rather cavalier fashion, I 'gave away' the rest of the band. I said to Gerry Bath "Have a band Gerry, it's called the Galleon". He got Clive Taylor in and changed the name to his own (revived) Climax Jazz

ern boehm system clarinet. The former came from Roy Coombes who used to 'sit in' with a rehearsal band run by Clive and Jill Whittingham, which eventually developed into Alice's Wonderland Band. Roy played a bass sax (whatever

The band performing at the Bristol Bridge Inn on the 4th May 1982. Back Row L to R: Robin Wood, Step Whitehead, Derek Lawrence, Tony Fennell, Alan Scott, Gus Gander and Henry. Front Row: Andy Leggett, Frank Fennell and Nick Cooper.

Band. Clive stayed but the rest dropped out one by one except Jed Collard who now had a sousaphone. By 1964 his band featured two trumpets, one of whom was Norman Thatcher, the other being Clive Whittingham. They were established at the Bathurst on Thursday nights. As most of the band were on holiday for two weeks in July, my new band was given the spot.

By that time I had acquired a baritone sax, as well as a mod-

became of it?) on a stand adapted from the lever and selector from an Austin Seven gearbox. He used to park the instrument leaning forward- that is in first gear. At the beginning of a number he would select second gear and progress through the 'gate' as he warmed to the task. When really into it he would slide effortlessly into top gear and the whole band would be cruising. Once he went into reverse by mistake with musically disastrous consequences. Fortunately no-one was seriously injured!

Roy had an Alladin's Cave of old instruments, many of which he had had the great good fortune to obtain from the University when they cleared out the attic of Goldney House. Besides the baritone sax, I also bought a bass clarinet and alto and tenor saxes from Roy. The baritone came in useful as an alternative bass for the band, and second reed parts were incorporated into early Ellington arrangements.

The new band needed a name. The name Bootblacks came from the New Orleans Bootblacks, a recording band led by Johnny Dodds for Victor in 1926. A residency at the much sought after Ship Inn, Redcliffe, began on October 1st 1964. Dick Farler, now my brother-in-law, had joined on second trumpet and Brian Mann on clarinet and tenor sax. The opening night was graced with a guest appearance of John R.T. Davies, then with the Temperance Seven and nowadays famous for his superb transfers of '78' records to CD.

The only night when the room was free at the Ship was a Thursday, which unfortunately clashed with Gerry Bath's gig at the Bathurst. In an act of generosity, Gerry closed his residency, leaving us without competition. His time came, however, when he secured the first residency at the Old Duke, by which time his band was called the Okeh Rhythm Kings.

Very soon after opening at the Ship, the band was augmented by Brian Huggett, (clarinet, alto and my baritone sax), leaving me free to play a continuous bass line. I soon added sousaphone to my arsenal of instruments. Everyone in the band agreed that it would be good to record the band. Stan Strickland recorded us at the Ship on 9th and 16th February, 1965 but the sessions produced insufficient passable material for a long playing album. By the time we recorded the remaining tracts Brian Mann and (Boots) Griffiths had moved to London and were replaced by Henry Phillpotts and Bernie Attridge. Terry Fry also left and Ron Brown came in on trombone. This line-up completed the album on the 7th of June and was issued as a limited edition of 99 copies, under the title "Vintage Jazz at the Ship Inn". I heard recently that a copy had changed hands for £25!

In November 1965 I joined Spencer's Washboard Kings. Three months later, after a tour of Belgium, Denmark and Sweden (three weeks, and over 9000 miles, in a clapped out Commer van) I packed it in because I was losing money! In March 1966 I returned to Bristol and the Bootblacks, still at the Ship, which had been kept going by Nick Cooper and Wayne Chandler.

Wayne had replaced Bernie Attridge when the latter gave up banjo and changed to string bass. Eventually Bernie left the U.K. for New Orleans where he still makes a living playing jazz.

I took up the bass position in a band which was now well known enough to attract some fine musicians, including two trombonists who were with the BBC Training Orchestra, at that time based in Bristol. These chaps arranged a recording session on the 25th September 1966 at Christchurch Hall, Clifton. The BBC engineers made a good job of it. I suppose we should have recorded "What a Little Moonlight Can Do"!

The band gradually expanded to a sixteen piece big band. From mid 1967 onwards I was working with various groups. A summer season with Spencer's was followed by a pantomime with the New Vaudeville band, then in 1968, till early in 1969, with Adge Cutler and the Wurzels. The Ship was demolished late in 1967 and the Bootblacks moved to the Quay Head Restaurant. A change of name to the Henry Davies Jazz Orchestra followed. I played with them whenever I was free but after a year or so the band was taken over by Pete Tomkins and renamed the Bristol Jazz Orchestra.

The music of the Wurzels was fun but of insufficient content to satisfy me. Encouraged by 'Gomez' Cooper, a 'Bix' style cornet/trumpet player, with whom I had worked with the New Vaudeville Band, I reformed an eight piece vintage hot band. At first called the Vintage Jazz Orchestra, to avoid confusion with the still extant Bootblacks, it soon took on the old name Henry's Bootblacks.

40

Besides 'Gomez', the band members were: Pete Kendall, trombone; Tom Timms and Nick Cooper, reeds; (Gus) Gander, sousaphone; Robin A. Wood, banjo; Basil Wright, drums, and yours truly on the piano. A few pub gigs were done in summer 1968 and by the autumn we had a residency at the Golden Q Club and a little later another at the Old Granary. The latter, though short lived, was both enjoyable and memorable for the comedy numbers which we would rehearse at Robin's house in the afternoon before the gig. Hopes that this band could turn full time were dashed when 'Gomez' emigrated to the USA where he still leads a successful show band.

The Fennell brothers, Frank and Tony, and Derek Lawrence (trumpet) brought new life to the Bootblacks in the early 1970s. A residency at the Pour House in King Street was augmented by gigs at the Granary and the Bell in Bath. I was also a member of the Pigsty Hill Light Orchestra and the Panama Jazz Band, an outfit led by pianist Robin Wood (an ex pupil of mine and not to be confused with R.A.Wood above) in this period and after a Radio Bristol broadcast in 1976 the Bootblacks broke up. I suppose this was inevitable at the time. Not only was I still gigging with the Panama and, increasingly, with Fred Wedlock, I was also studying full time at Bristol University.

In 1981 (Gus) Gander suggested reviving the ten piece Bootblacks. As Derek and the Fennells were quite keen, I gave it a go. An early residency at the Bristol Bridge Inn led to a BBC broadcast recording for Radio 2 in September 1982 and our "High Society" album was produced in 1984, financed by public subscription among Bristol jazz fans, all of whom received a reasonable return on their outlay. The line-up at this time was: Derek Lawrence and Bob Mickleburgh, trumpets; Mike (Step) Whitehead, trombone; Frank Fennell, Nick Cooper and Andy Leggett, reeds; Robin A. Wood, banjo/guitar; (Gus) Gander, sousa/string bass; Tony Fennell, later Dick Thomas and finally, Bob Watkins, drums, and me on piano and odd bits of third trumpet.

Periodic Sunday lunchtime sessions at the Old Duke were among the most enjoyable of the many engagements the band played. In 1987 we recorded the "Hullabaloo" album for the United States Stomp Off jazz label. The line up had changed somewhat by this time. Frank Fennell had been replaced by the wayward and mercurial Richard White. Richard, a brilliant 'hot' jazzman, played clarinet, bass clarinet, C melody and tenor (as well as piano, banjo and washboard when required). The lead trumpet was played by David Ford, who took over from Derek Lawrence and who was in turn replaced by Harvey Baigent. My nephew Joe Farler replaced Robin on banjo and guitar when the latter changed to tuba, replacing (Gus). Robin left in 1988 and was replaced by the present sousaphone player, Mike Lancaster. The redoubtable John Watson came in on drums. The rest of the band members were the same as on the "High Society" album. Sometimes we augmented into a 'Hot Dance Orchestra' by adding Will Goodchild on violin.

The band had been used by the BBC for regular broadcast recordings at Christchurch studio until the music department at Bristol was closed. The Christchurch studio was sold and the staff transferred to Birmingham in 1991. Work for the band dried up after that, and although still in existence, public appearances of Henry's Bootblacks are now rare. Because there is a pool of first rate 'hot' players upon whose services I can call, these intermittent engagements are eagerly awaited by the jazz cognoscenti.

Henry Davies

JAZZMEN ANONYMOUS

Playing Kenny Ball style jazz this band performed at The Little Thatch Country Club,Whitchurch, and various other venues. The band had a regular spot at the Thatch, attracting a full house virtually every Friday night. Things went very well for us until one night, for some unknown reason the only person who turned up to hear us play was a regular. He had come to hear us play our singalong medley (Pack up your Troubles in your Old Kit Bag, etc).As it turned out, very prophetic. The then landlord decided he wasn't going to pay us, and during the ensuing polite discourse regarding the various merits of the case, his wife tried to add her compelling reasoning with the soda fountain. That was our last night.

I went on to play in various local trios and quartets and frequently played alongside John Gill in the Kenny Scott Band. I met Ian(Flurge)Appleyard during this time and occasionally deputised for him when he found himself double booked. On one such occasion he had been hired by a car rally club to play for their evening BBQ in a tent in the middle of a field, somewhere near Pucklechurch. After the day's packed events there was an evening audience of six and an abundance of free beer. The electricity generator ran out of fuel so we all got paid and went home.

I stopped band work for a few years to make time for cabaret shows and compere work in various clubs, pubs and holiday camps. My return to band music came when I joined the Parkway Big Band in 1975 as lead trumpet for a couple of years. Later I joined Chantilly Lace for two years.

Being a musician and married are not necessarily compatible and it was this which caused me to withdraw from the scene in 1979. After a break of 16 years I have started to play again on an intermittent basis with the idea of starting regular band work again.

Regular members of Jazzmen Anonymous were: Alan Scott, clarinet/tenor sax; John Hopkins, trombone; John Gill, banjo/guitar; Jim Watkins, drums, and myself leading on trumpet.

Terry Black

K T TRAD LADS

all aged 15/16 Years 1961 - 1963

As the title suggests we were all still at school when we started in 1961. Keith Tippet, Mike Milton, Martin Nicholas and myself were musicians in the school brass band where we received formal music training. Keith Tippet was, I think, also a grade 5 pianist. I took several examinations for the Royal Bandsman's College of Music. The school at which I attended gained a new music master at about the same time that I was principal soloist with the school band and the Bristol Youth Band. The poor man, having no love of brass, rated me as a 'good listener'.

The K T Trad Lads, under the watchful eye of Eric Condell's

A very early 1960s photograph of the KT Trad Lads in action. L to R: Mike Milton, Keith Tippet, Bobby Chard, Eric Condell, Martin Nicholas and Terry Black.

father as manager, played Temperance Seven and Kenny Ball style music at various venues, including the Towns Talk and Paradise Motel.

A recording was also made for BBC radio for Children's Hour. We used to go regularly to the Crown and Dove to listen to Keith Box and others.

Whatever happened to the Trad Lads? The band continued playing until 1963. Keith Tippet went on to play regular sessions at the Dugout Club with Bobby Chard and a flautist whose name I cannot remember. Martin Nicholas, Mike Milton and Eric Condell retired from music. Keith Tippet is currently playing extremely modern jazz at various venues and lectures regularly in the Summer School at Dartington Manor.

Band members were: Keith Tippet, piano; Mike Milton, trombone; Martin Nicholas, brass bass; Eric Condell, banjo; Bobby Chard, drums, and myself on trumpet.

Terry Black

THE MAX EVANS QUARTET

The band was formed in 1963 and led by Andy Bartlett on clarinet. The original line-up was Russ Morgan on piano, (Spud) Taylor bass, and myself on drums and vocals.

The quartet first played at the Dug Out club in Park Row and was there for three years. From then on the band became a Dance/Jazz quartet, playing at many social clubs on a monthly basis.

There were several changes of members over the decade of the bands existence, Russ Morgan died and was replaced by Geoff Roberts and later by Ray Winters. (Spud) Taylor turned professional and was replaced by Ron Cox. Randy Bartlett died and Don Burnell came into the Band on reeds.

Originally the band's musical style was based on the Benny Goodman Quartet. However it gradually developed to encompass numbers as varied as "Air on a G String" to Count Basie's "Flight of the Foo Birds".

While playing at the Dug Out club a regular visitor would sit and listen, this was before he formed his own band, the now internationally famous Keith Tippet!

All bands have their high and low moments. Nothing goes wrong on New Years Eve? The Max Evans Quartet was playing a New Years dance on the former Lightship in Bathhurst Basin, and everything was going according to plan. The dancers needed no encouragement, the dance floor being crowded for every dance, and all intent on seeing in the New Year in style. Everyone who has attended a New Years bash knows the time honoured procedure, the ten-second countdown to midnight and the singing of Old Lang Syne, followed by hugs, handshakes, kisses and mayhem! On this occasion the best laid plans of mice and men didn't quite work. The master of ceremonies called every one onto the floor, consulted his watch and began the countdown. 10. 9. 8........the band were poised, 7. 6. 5....... dear old Randy took a deep breath, put clarinet to mouth 4. 3. 2. I.......and came in with HAPPY BIRTHDAY TO YOU !!!! During the ensuing moments several things happened. The dancers stood with blank expressions, the pianist tried desperately to play the right tune, the master of ceremonies was totally lost for words and what the rest of the band said to Randy will not be printed here, but is still well remembered and in no way complimentary. Anyway we still got paid.

Dave Hibberd

THE NEW CHICAGOANS
1966 - 1992

Sometime in 1965 Reg Quantrill, John 'Hoppy' Hopkins and I began visiting the Dugout Club in Park Row, Bristol, to have an after-hours beer and to listen to the Max Evans Quartet, a little group led by Dave Hibberd. We would take our instruments and sit in for a number or two, so that the augmented group became a standard jazz band. After some weeks it became apparent that these were no longer random jam sessions, but the makings of a new band. By April 1966 the New Chicagoans were formed under the leadership of

44

The New Chicagoans performing at the Top Rank Ballroom in 1969. L to R: Ron Cox, bass; John Hopkins, trombone; Dave Hibberd, drums; Mike Cocks, leader, trumpet; Russ Morgan, piano and Randy Bartlett, clarinet.

Dave Hibberd. The original line up was Mike Cocks, trumpet; Hoppy, trombone; Randy Bartlett, clarinet; Russ Morgan, piano; Reg Quantrill, guitar/banjo; Graham (Spud) Taylor, bass, and Dave Hibberd, drums and leader.

Our first job was promoted by Mike Bevan and Eric Clift who had recently started running regular Sunday sessions at the Old Mill, Bathhampton. This took place on the 10th April 1966. Two days later, we were to be found at the Beaufort Hunt, Chipping Sodbury, where we were to remain in residence for six months. Then in October 1966 the band moved to the New Passage Hotel at Pilning, where we were all but adopted by the formidable landlady, Molly Bracey. She was reputed to have been a vaudeville artist in her younger days and amongst her valued possessions was a fine grand piano. Nobody was allowed to touch it unless they had suffered an audition. Russ's audition lasted about eight bars before

Molly's stentorian voice announced "You'll do, my darling!".

Every month or so we invited that fine guitarist Jack Toogood along as a guest. Jack had more or less given up session work and was concentrating on teaching, but it was these nights at the New Passage that probably encouraged him to re-appear more often on the local jazz scene.

During 1968 things started to go sour. Russ, who had been blind since childhood and suffered from pleurisy, became seriously ill and for several months the band had to use deputy pianists, usually Dave Collett or John Hooper and on odd occasions John Critchinson who went on to be part of the Ronnie Scott group. Then the advent of the breathalyser put paid to the New Passage. The hotel was about twelve miles out of town and suddenly too far from Bristol for people to drive. Molly didn't want us to leave, but there was little point in playing to an empty house. So the New Chicagoans were without a home.

For the next couple of years we played odd jobs at the Granary, including one with our first 'name' guest, George Chisholm. But tragedy struck. In December 1969 Russ died, to be followed in November 1971 by the equally sad death (by drowning) of Randy. This knocked the stuffing out of us and to make matters worse, if that was possible, the Max Evans Quartet had been doing more and more jobs which were clashing with the band's potential bookings. So there had been a gradual parting of the ways and we found ourselves on the verge of breaking up.

After a few months of inactivity Hoppy was instrumental in

The band photographed at the City Docks in July 1975 (note the cargo boat). L to R: Dave Millman, piano; Brian Huggett, reeds; Mike Cocks, trumpet; Reg Quantrill, guitar and banjo; Roy Smith, drums; John (Hoppy) Hopkins, trombone, and John Macey, bass.

persuading me that we should start playing again. So we reformed after a fashion under my nominal leadership, but without a regular line-up. During this period we were lucky to have the help of Dave Millman and Brian Huggett from the Severn Jazzmen, who did sterling service with us and with-

out whose help we would never have survived. We played regularly in such places as the Parkway Social Club, Hunters Hall at Kingscote, near Dursley, the Horsefair, and Clifton Rugby Club. It was at the Bristol Fashion that we celebrated our 10th birthday with a party to which we invited all the musicians who had ever played with, or sat in with, the New Chicagoans. The idea was to get them all to play during the course of the evening, but so many turned up that we could scarcely fit them all in, let alone get them all to play!

After nearly four years at the Malt and Hops from June 1977 to January 1981 (and in 1978 with a very short spell at the Portcullis, Chipping Sodbury), the new Chicagoans finally settled into their regular Friday night spot at the Old Duke. The date was the 27th April 1979, not too long after John Stone had replaced Kon Aniol as landlord of what had already become a very well-established jazz pub. By this time the personnel was settling into a fairly regular line-up: Graham Slann, trombone; Alan Taylor, tenor/clarinet and tin whistle; Don Burnell, tenor/clarinett; Les Drake, piano; Roy Smith, drums; Geoff Weldrake, bass, and myself on trumpet. It was this band which had the pleasure of accompanying the almost legendary Doc Cheatham at the Old Duke.

I had got to know Doc well through several visits to the Nice Jazz Festival on the French Riviera. Doc was a regular favourite there, and he would come most days and give chats to us Brits at our lunchtime drinking hole, although he himself rarely drank. On one occasion I had him to myself, and it was with some trepidation that I asked if he would be willing to guest with the band when he was next in the U.K. Doc assured me he would be delighted and honoured (he was always the perfect gentleman!). And so it happened. We only advertised the event by word of mouth (although I was invited to give it a plug on Radio Bristol's Jazz Tempo programme) but the evening turned out to be an unbelievable success. We not only had our normal crowd there, but people were coming in off the street, and realising that something special was afoot, were staying put. By the interval people were standing on the tables because there was no room on the floor, and the band couldn't get off the stage. Doc played every number except the first and he would have played that if I hadn't suggested that he heard the band first. He blew up such a storm that people are still talking about the occasion to this day.

It was also at the Old Duke that we acquired an unofficial fan club. An ever increasing band of Bristol University students under the leadership of one Grey (we never did discover his surname) would come every Friday with the intention of drinking the pub dry and thoroughly enjoying themselves. They soon took to wearing button badges exalting various members of the band and especially the unlikely personage of Alan Taylor. The latter's badges became so prolific that one was actually spotted on the London Underground with the legend "ALAN TAYLOR IS GOD"!

Over the years we've had the pleasure of playing alongside many of the country's top jazz musicians, some of whom have become firm friends. Apart from Doc, who of course was American, and George Chisholm mentioned earlier, there have been regular visitations from such notables as Danny Moss, John Barnes, Roy Williams, Bruce Turner, Alan Elsdon, Cy Laurie, John Wurr and Harry Gold. It was to Harry that I suggested a duet with Alan Taylor on bass sax and tin whistle! Harry was delighted with the idea and declared that this for him would be a first. He was in his eightieth year!

The New Chicagoans started out very much under the influence of the Alex Welsh band. In those early days many vis-

iting groups were to be heard in the Bristol area, and the Welsh band was no exception. So we had ample opportunities to hear our idols in the flesh. But as time went on it seemed there were too many groups in the Bristol area playing a similar brand of dixieland jazz, and I felt it was time to move on a bit. No one was playing much mainstream jazz of the small group swing variety, so it seemed that this was the way to go. In the end we compromised between the two styles and I think we did it with some success.

However, after fronting the band for 26 years, I decided to call it a day. There were several reasons for this, but two stand out above all. Firstly, I felt the band at that time had run out of steam and was no longer going anywhere. This was due in part to some enforced personnel changes, which meant we could no longer use some of our better arrangements, but mainly my fault in that I was losing my enthusiasm for jazz generally. Secondly, and this ties in with my last comment, I was stagnating as a player - and had been for a few years. In fact it was only my wife who had stopped me from packing up four years earlier (she said I would be like a bear with a sore head if I stopped playing, and she was probably right!). However, by September 1992 I had had enough and finally decided to bring to an end 36 years of trumpeting.

I look back on those years, the last 26 years in particular, with some satisfaction. I don't miss playing at all now, but at least I've done it, and done it with a fine band. I only hope the New Chicagoans can carry on for many years to come and continue to be a band full of fun and exuberance. I wish them well.

To finish, here is a complete list of all the musicians who have been regular members of the band up to the end of August 1992:-

Trumpet; Mike Cocks.
Trombone; John Hopkins, Tony Osborne, Graham Slann, Ron Brown.
Clarinet & Saxes;Randy Bartlett, Brian Huggett, Alan Taylor, Don Burnell, Andy Leggett.

Piano; Russ Morgan, Dave Millman, Les Drake, Ray Winter, Alan Hurley
Drums; Dave Hibberd, Trevor Ottolang, Basil Wright, Reg Harrison, Roy Smith, Brian Osborne.
Bass; Graham 'Spud' Taylor, Ron Cox, Mike Nealon, Bernie Attridge, John Macey, Geoff Weldrake.
Guitar and banjo; Reg Quantrill, Wayne Chandler.
Managers; Geoff Sheppard, Mike Nichols.

I hope I haven't missed anybody out, but at the time of writing the band has been going for 32 years, and after that period the memory can play tricks. So, if you're not on the list, please accept my apologies; the error wasn't intentional!

Mike Cocks

OKEH RHYTHM KINGS

If I remember rightly the Okeh Rhythm Kings were formed in the bar of the White Bear in Kingsdown, Bristol.

The musicians had been rehearsing in the upstairs room every Monday night for some time under the leadership of pianist Gerry Bath. On Monday night in January 1966, it was thought that the band was ready to launch themselves onto the Bristol Jazz Scene. The Band comprised Clive Whittingham, trumpet; Clive Taylor, Clarinet/alto; Pete Kendall, trombone; Martin Ashman, banjo; Cliff Brown, drums, and myself, sousaphone.) My wife Hazel was doing the vocals. After taking the decision to look for a suitable venue, a debate ensued concerning what we should call ourselves. Gerry Bath had a long history of leading bands, including Climax, which many leading local jazz musicians had been with at some time or other and naturally could see no reason why the name Climax should not be chosen.

Another line of thought was that a new name for the band might be more appropriate. After about four more pints we settled for the Okeh (after the record label) Rhythm Kings. The trouble was that none of us could spell the word 'rhythm' but we decided to worry about that later! We were all keen on the so called 'classics' style and drew mainly on early Ellington, Oliver and Morton Bands for our material, and together with Hazel, a great Bessie Smith devotee, we worked hard to accumulate around eighty 'head arrangements'. It was rumoured that Clive Whittingham had the biggest repertoire in town. This was refuted by his wife Jill (Alice) when she joined the band later.

The band got its first regular job at the Bear in the Hotwells Road in February 1966 and managed to outnumber the audience for eight consecutive weeks before we got the sack. During this period we made firm friends with Mike and Sheila Edkin. They volunteered to manage the band and look out for a new venue. Also, I believe, we saw the founding of the Alligator Jug Thumpers when Cliff Brown formed a 'band within a band'. The line-up was Cliff, jug and aspirin bottle; Clive Taylor, alto; Martin Ashman, banjo, and Gerry Bath, piano. I played washboard and 'hands cupped over the mouth'. I couldn't afford a Kazoo!

Cliff left the band in March to develop the Jug Thumpers along with Q. Williams and Barry Back, and I remember them bringing the house down at a packed concert at the Colston Hall with their brand of music and humour. Gerry Gittens replaced Cliff Brown on drums and shortly afterwards Robin Wood replaced Martin Ashman on banjo.

The Band went back to rehearsals every Monday at the White Bear until Mike and Sheila announced that they had secured

A group photograph of the OKEH Rhythm Kings taken close to the Observatory, Clifton Down, about 1968. L to R: Jed Collard, Clive Taylor, Pete Kendall, Jerry Gittens, Clive Whittingham, Gerry Bath and Robin Wood.

a Saturday night at the Old Duke in King Street for a trial period.

The band was offered a smallish room upstairs, free of charge, provided we swept up and collected glasses after the show (there was no bar in the room). Kon and Alma Aniol ran the Duke in those days and we were delighted to be able to play at such a good location near the centre of Bristol. This was April 1967 and I believe the Rhythm Kings were the first band to play regularly at the Old Duke. Mike and Sheila manned the door. We charged two shillings and sixpence (12.5 pence) to come in and we were ready.

From the opening night the place was packed (I did say the room was smallish). It was normal for Mike and Sheila to open the doors at 8.00 p.m. and having to refuse people admission by 8.30 p.m.

I have many fond memories of that period, particularly during the summers when the windows were wide open and glancing down to see dozens of people dancing in King Street below. I remember one night during the summer when a young man, having failed to gain entry at the door, shinned up the temporary scaffolding outside and scrambled through the open window earning a tremendous cheer from the crowd. This feat of nerve and agility was truly remarkable because he held a pint and hadn't spilled a drop!

The size of the room made it impossible not to develop a good rapport with the audience. We devised a regular Charleston dancing competition adjudicated by Mike and Sheila. First prize - a Rhythm Kings L.P., second prize, - Two Rhythm Kings L.Ps and so on. We also did the occasional 'swap' with other bands, particularly the Zenith Hot Stompers who were based in Birmingham.

I will never forget the time the Red Onion Jazzband from Melbourne, Australia, first played the Duke. Nigel Hunt, who knew the band whilst he lived in Melbourne, told us that they were on a European Tour and were shortly coming to England. Nigel reckoned, judging from the last time he had heard them, they were very promising but 'as rough as a badger's arse'!

It was around 7.30 p.m. when a shattered old white van, billowing thick black smoke from the exhaust, pulled up outside the door in Queen Charlotte Street. The driver, a scruffy 'schoolboy' with outrageously long hair, walked round to the back of the van and yanked open the door. One by one six more scruffy 'schoolboys' scrambled out of the van clutching cases and various bits of a drum kit. The driver, struggling to lock the back door, called out in a very broad Australian accent, "Sorry we're a bit lite mite, only we came strite from Poland." Could this gang of adolescent antipodean hippies be the Red Onions? (The old man of the band claimed to be 26). I, and a few others, doubted whether they would be fit or strong enough to open their cases let alone play! Anyone who was at the Duke that night will confirm that the band was sensational. We found out later that the band had secured a free passage from Australia by playing in the ship's ballroom from 8 p.m. to 4.00 a.m., six nights a week for the six week journey. By the time they got to England they had polished up the rough edges and were raring to go.

In December 1968 Pete Kendall and Robin Wood left the Okeh Band in order to join Henry's Bootblacks, and were replaced by Jim Scadding, on trombone, who is Hazel's cousin, and Jill Whittingham who is Clive's wife.

It was February 1969 that the Band left the Duke in order to fulfil a contract to play for 36 weeks at the Old Granary. This happened because the contract forbade us to play on a regular basis at any venue within a square mile of the Granary itself.

The Old Granary, at that time, was open seven days a week from 8.00 p.m. to 2.00 a.m. (11 p.m. Sundays), engaging the best bands in the country. The Rhythm Kings initially had the Tuesday night spot as 'warm up' band between 8.00 and 11.00 p.m. after which the star attractions would perform. It was not long, however, before management found it too costly to employ 'named' bands throughout the week and for many weeks the Rhythm Kings did the show on their own , attracting good crowds for a Tuesday night.

When the contract expired, the band moved back to the Old Duke. Gerry Gittens left the band in 1970 to be replaced by Bob 'Ashley' Phillips, who just happened to be Jimmy Scadding's brother-in-law.

It was May 1970 that the Rhythm Kings were chosen to represent the U.K. (along with Keith Smith's Climax Jazz Band from London) at the Dunkirk International Jazz Festival. It was an exhilarating experience mixing and playing with bands from all over Europe, the star attractions being Bill Coleman and Albert Nicholas.

All good things must come to an end and the band played its last engagement at Cheddar in the summer of 1971. The band did leave a legacy, however, by means of a ten inch L.P. recorded by Stan Strickland at the House of Sound in Bristol, and released on Gosport Sounds label in May 1968. Only 99 copies were pressed because (a) you avoided paying some kind of tax (a typical Gerry Bath ploy), and (b) we didn't want to get lumbered with a load of records that we couldn't get rid of. We sold out within days of release.

The tunes recorded were; "Steamboat Stomp", "Ford Engine Movements"*, "Everybody Loves My Baby", "He Likes It Slow"**, "Charleston", "Zulu's Ball", "Jelly Bean Blues",

"Black Mountain Blues"*, and "Cake Walking Babies"**.

* Hazel Collard vocal
** Duet Hazel and Jed Collard

I am delighted to be able to tell you that I have recently been informed by my fan that it has now become a collector's item. That is of course, if my memory serves me correctly!

Jed Collard

SEVERN JAZZMEN

The Severn Jazzmen was formed in 1967 but some members of the band had performed together as the Steamboat Stompers and the K City Six. The Steamboat Stompers played at the Black Horse, Thornbury from April 1964 until March 1967. The line up was Dave Millman, piano; C. Hemmings, drums; D. Bliss, trombone; R. Riddiford, bass; A. Dodds, trumpet; Kate Heany, vocals and later Kate Bliss.

The Severn Jazzmen played in the Bear, Hotwells, before starting at the Old Duke in King Street, being the first band to play in the downstairs bar in 1968. The band personnel at that time was P. Kendall, trombone; Rex Baker, trumpet; Brian Huggett, reeds; R. Riddiford, bass; Bill Banner, guitar and banjo, and myself on piano.

In September 1979 the Severn Jazzmen were recorded on the "Jazz at The Duke" record with a track "Lester Leaps In".

The musicians on that occasion were Dave Millman, piano; Ian [Flurge] Appleyard, trumpet; Brian Huggett, clarinet and alto sax; John Hopkins, trombone; John Viner, guitar and banjo; Bob Riddiford, bass and Gordon Mogridge, drums.

There have been many other musicians who have played with the band for long or shorter periods, apologies to any whom I have ommitted from the following list: Bill Billet, Maurice Everson, bass; John Watson, Reg Harrison, Roger Wells, drums; Pete Harrison, reeds; Norman Hill, trumpet.

Well known guest musicians and singers have played with the band, including Acker Bilk, Alan Elsdon, Roy Williams, Danny Moss, Digby Fairweather, Beryl Bryden and Rusty Taylor.

The general style of the band is Dixieland and the influences from the numerous great jazz musicians of that period in jazz.

There are innumerable stories of things that have happened on our travels or at the Old Duke over the years. One that readily comes to mind and takes the biscuit was when a punter asked Flurge if he knew "Mother Kelly's Doorstep". The reply was, "Yes, and I've been sick on it many a night"!

Our present line up is A. Bramley, trombone; M. Williams, cornet; Brian Huggett, reeds; [Cass] Casswell, bass; J. Widdowson, drums, and yours truly on piano.

Compiled from information supplied by Dave Millman
Editors

SOCIETY JAZZ BAND

The band was formed in the very early 60s with the following personnel:
Dave Kingston (Leader), Trumpet; Derek Joynson, Clarinet; John Rossiter, Trombone; David Jackson, Drums; Tony Beese, Banjo, and Bill Smith, Bass.

Early on the band had no fixed venue and played wherever they could get a gig! However, about this time the Bathurst Pub was opening with just one night devoted to Jazz. The Society Band collectively decided to take a chance and booked Friday nights, (at this time the Landlords did not pay the band, you had to pay a fee to hire the room and hope to make a profit on door takings at the end of the evening!) Adverts were placed in the Evening Post and the rest was in the lap of the Gods! The first few Fridays had patchy attendance, but none the less encouraging. With continued advertising the crowd began to build up nicely and pretty soon the place was packed out every Friday night. The Landlord even resorted to installing an early warning system to signal the arrival of any of the Boys in Blue. This consisted of a bell-push in the downstairs bar and a buzzer behind the upstairs bar. All these precautions were not really necessary as I do not recall any real trouble from what was always a very good natured crowd.

As always there were some changes in personnel, these included:
Alex Mills who was of West Indian parents but born in Bristol, and a very fine guitarist, joined us on trombone. Alex who was diabetic regretfully died some years later in the Bristol Royal Infirmary after an infection in his foot became gangrenous. Even the amputation of his leg failed to stop the spread of gangrene. He was a sad loss to the Bristol jazz scene.

Randy Bartlett replaced Derek on clarinet after a couple of years into the Bathurst residency. Randy was a fun character who played an Archie Semple style clarinet and was always the life and soul of the party.

Clive Johnson, clarinet, replaced Randy after about a year. Clive played, and still does a very fluid clarinet and remained with the band during the rest of my time with the Society Jazzband.

Randy Bartlett was also lost to the Bristol scene, a victim of a boating accident. He was lost overboard whilst sailing a small dingy single-handed in Poole Harbour.

The band played at many jazz venues throughout the area as well as in South Wales and Gloucestershire. They also bought a Jazz Club in Chipping Sodbury, playing every week for a number of years at the Beaufort Hunt in the main Street. This was also well attended with a regular gathering of jazz fans from that local area.

The musical style of the band was based on New Orleans roots with overtones of Armstrong, and even some Dixieland influences, not to mention the obligatory "Chime Blues"! There were even touches of Duke Ellington at times. A fan at the Bathurst, one Boris by name requested we do a jazz version of "Hear My Song Violetta", which we duly delivered the next week!

A couple of private recordings were made, but never issued to my knowledge.

Most original members of the band are still around and still playing. Bill Smith I believe emigrated to Canada in the early Seventies but I have been unable to verify this.

Tony Beese

TULANE

My first band was formed in the summer of 1960. The original members were Keith Box, clarinet; Guy Woodford, cornet; Sandy Miller, String/Bass; Mike Pugh, piano; Tony Beese, banjo; Dave Hibberd, drums, and Pete Child, trombone.

The first venue was the Bathurst Hotel, Wapping Road 1960 - 64. Then the Ship Inn, Redcliffe Hill 1964/5-67, returning to the Bathurst 1968-1970/1. The band also did a brief stint at the Bear Hotel in Hotwells in the late 1960s and in the early 1970s at the George and Railway, Temple Meads.

I left the band in August 1968 to go to college and university, and Tulane was taken over by banjoist Bob Phoenix, who changed the name to the Phoenix Jazzmen.

During my time with the early Tulane several musicians came and went as Tulane edged closer to the black New Orleans revivalist style of jazz I sought. Crucial to this development were the clarinetist Trevor Bricker and pianist Fred Manners, who were later joined by Tim Newman on trumpet, and Richie Bryant on drums. Both Trevor and Fred took a great deal of persuading to join Tulane, on what might be called ideological grounds. They felt that their music would be inevitably compromised by playing in public, as it were, for money - albeit for quite modest amounts. But I needed those guys, so I just badgered away at them over several months and finally they agreed to join up. Trevor was a quite serious asthma sufferer, which often caused him great distress. A good guy and a beautiful Lewis-style clarinet player, he died, tragically in 1974.

Other players who were important to the style of the band were Mike (Whiskers) Williams, Mick Daniels and Dennis Beaumont on drums; Bernie Attridge, banjo and string/bass; who now lives in New Orleans. The arrival of the rhythmic string/bass man, Pete Hunt made a big difference to the quality of the back line. Bob Phoenix and Jay Hawkins, on tenor banjos.

The Tulane Band at the Bathurst Hotel in 1960. L to R: Pete Child, Sandy Miller, Guy Woodford, Dave Hibberd, Keith Box and Tony Beese.

53

Back in those days the bands ran their own clubs on pub premises, accountable only to the landlord, rather than the battalions of accountants and actuaries employed these days by the big breweries. We charged half a crown or 'three bob' entrance and everybody danced, drank and had a good time.

Sometime in the early 70s (I wasn't in Bristol at the time) the Phoenix band folded and the musicians I had employed moved off to join other bands. Richie Bryant had gone to London to play with the Lightfoot band I think, and then with Acker Bilk. Tim Newman teamed up with Keith Box and so on.

Around 1976 or 77 I joined the Keith Box band and worked with them for a few years playing in the cellar bar of the Crown in St Nicholas Market and later at the Bristol Bridge Inn. Then in 1980 I decided to re-form Tulane.

By this time, finding the people I needed in Bristol alone was just not going to be possible. The style of music I mentioned above, based on the 'black' New Orleans revival of the 1940s through to the present day was not generally what most local musicans either understood or wanted to get involved with. Based on a disciplined ensemble approach to the music, there is absolutely no room for stars who want only to demonstrate technical fireworks, if you know what I mean. The idiom also has specific musical components within its repetoire, like spirituals, parade tunes and dirges, etc. When I looked around in 1980 most of the bands were playing British traditional or music modelled on 1920s Chicago sounds after what we call Morton/Oliver style. So it was necessary to look also outside Bristol and Bath.

Norman Thatcher (who had played briefly with the early Tulane band) came down from Gloucester and he brought with him a beautiful drum man called Colin Bushell. Dave Gray, a Londoner living in Bristol, came in on string/bass and Jay Hawkins took on the banjo seat. Johnny Cartlidge (another early Tulane man) brought his clarinet, and an old social friend of mine, Enoch Hunt played the piano. Enoch

was no virtuoso, but he played the right chords and kept it simple - his music fitted the band.

We took up residency at the Bristol Bridge Inn until around 1983 or 84 until the owners told us that time was up. All the jazz at the Bridge had to give way to what the kids wanted and the rock bands moved in. Pity, really, because the Bridge had a late licence and was always fairly relaxed. A lot of drinking was done during that time! Nigel Hunt replaced Norman Thatcher, Mick Daniels took over from Colin. A superb bass player, Roger White joined the band and when Jay left, a Birmingham man, Brian (Smiley) Helliwell took over, and brought his guitar with him as well.

From the Bridge we moved up to the White Hart on Park Row who wanted to try something to pull in some customers. We were joined up there by a swing combo which featured Geoff Nichols among others. When the accountants closed this scene down after about nine months we had nowhere to go. Then John Stone rang me and offered the band a fortnightly spot in the Old Duke. There was a kind of irony about this because Trevor and I were among the first to enquire about putting jazz on at the Duke back in the mid sixties, when the pub was just an end of the street bar with practically no drinkers.

Tulane played in the Duke from 1985, I think until 13th December 1995, a year after the pub's new owners had decided to change things round and replace a lot of the jazz with .....? I'm afraid the guys in my band lost that gig because I, personally, had made myself unpopular with the new management, but that's a story all on its own.

Times at the Duke were good for the Tulane Band. The crowds were good, the band's repetoire was expanded a great deal and I think we played good black New Orleans jazz. In 1987 Tulane represented Bristol City Council on the 40th anniversary celebrations in Bordeaux, France. We also did lots of gigs in different parts of the country, including a tour of northern clubs, and the Groningen Festival in Holland. In

1997 I was able to fulfil a personal ambition by taking the band to play gigs in Prague. Tulane has also featured a number of times at the largely New Orleans Bude Jazz Festival.

The last line up of the band was Roger White, string/bass; Tom Whittingham, a fine New Orleans drummer (and trombone player), Bill Scott from Malvern, Worcs, banjo; Geoff Roberts, piano; Nigel Hunt, trumpet; Hugh Roberts, a brilliant clarinet and tenor sax man and myself. Also for over a year we were helped out by Dave Collett, who everybody knows, on piano, and Wayne Chandler, who did a stint with us on banjo. At the 'away' gigs and festivals we had lovely players like Mike Lunn from Cumbria on piano, Mac McDonald from Devon on banjo and guitar, and Manchester trumpet man, Derek Winters. I don't know what the future is for Tulane. Maybe that's it. We'll see.

Tulane has made one 10 inch LP (in 1968) comprising 99 copies. Two audio tapes were made in 1992 and 1994. A recording of the band for BBC Radio Bristol was made in 1982 under the supervision of the then DJ, Mike Bevan.

Pete Child

THE 1970s

ALICE'S WONDERLAND BAND

Clive and I decided to form Alice's Wonderland Band in 1974 with the aim of recreating the Classic Jazz sounds of the 1920s and the music from the Dance Band Days of the 1930s. We aimed to have a band which came across as being 'fun' and include musicians in the line-up who would be good players but not prima donnas or fanatics to purism.

Our line-up at present consists of Clive Whittingham, cornet; Tom Whittingham, trombone, euphonium, washboard and whistles; Hugh Roberts, clarinet and tenor sax; myself, banjo and vocals, and John 'The Bear' Massey, double bass.
In the past we have included musicians such as Jed Collard and Bobby Mickleburgh, trombone; Alan Taylor, Brian Huggett and Andy Leggett, clarinet and saxes; Brian Walker and Ken Fitzgerald, sousaphone; Roger Wells, Geoff Cook and Norman Thatcher, drums, and Quentin Reynolds, violin. In our original line up we had Robin Wood on piano and Gordon Smith on drums. We were all devastated when, in 1980, Gordon was killed in a car accident. He had such a wonderful personality and, apart from his drumming, he also sang and, in fact, can be heard on the "Jazz at the Duke" record singing "The Kings Horses."

For a while afterwards our son Tom, who was then only four-

A 1980s photo of Alice's Wonderland Band. Standing L to R: John Massey, Tom Whittingham, Clive Whittingham and Brian Huggett. Seated L to R: Robin Wood and Jill Whittingham.

teen years old played washboard with us. I think that probably makes him the youngest regular band member to ever have played at the Old Duke. Later, when he was able to drive at seventeen he took over as our drummer.

Originally we performed at The George and Railway, the Grosvenor Hotel, The Portland House in St Pauls (and that caused a riot!), and also The Sands nightclub in Whiteladies Road. Later, we returned to The Old Duke. (He used to be Old in those days, I'm not quite sure why he isn't today). Initially we were there on Monday evenings, then moved to Saturday and, eventually, Tuesdays where we stayed until the big disaster of 1995.

Our band is still going strong today with a regular Monday evening session at The Eagle Tavern in Old Market, the usual round of weddings, funerals and 60th birthday parties (why are there so many of those lately?) and, my favourite, the Jazz

Festivals which, fortunately, seem to be springing up every-where, especially during the Summer months.

As you can see, Alice's band has been around for over 25 years now and we are hoping to be around for a few more yet!

Jill Whittingham

Bath City performing as a Marching Band. L to R: Tom Whittingham, bass drum; Henry Davies, sousaphone; Andy Leggett, tenor sax; Roger Wells, snare drum: John Gill, banjo; Pete Martin, leader, trumpet; Nick Cooper, clarinet, and Step Whitehead, trombone.

BATH CITY JAZZ BAND

This Dixieland band originally from Bath, is included in this book because most of the musicians came from Bristol and were eventually based there. Led and formed by Pete Martin on trumpet-cornet, the original members were (Step) Whitehead, trombone; Dave Stone, reeds; Geoff Miller, bass; Alan Edwards, drums and Reg Quantrill, banjo/guitar/vocals.

The Bath City's first regular venue was the Entertainer Bar in the Fernley Hotel, Bath from 1978 to 1980. Then after two years at The Bell they secured a regular Saturday night berth at the Old Duke, King Street, Bristol from 1982 to 1995. Many other bands would have liked the Saturday slot in the Duke. However, there was a snag. From time to time Bath City had offers of more lucrative gigs on Saturday evenings and these could not be ignored. The landlord John Stone understood this and released them. This gave other bands the chance to play what was then a very popular gig.

Following John Stone's retirement the Saturday night spot ended with the Brewery's change of policy not to have jazz on Saturday nights. This ended Bath City's regular residency.

Changes of personnel over the years were as fol-

Bath City Jazz Band performing outside the Duke in the 1970s. L to R: Step Whitehead, John Gill, Pete Martin (leader), Alan Edwards, Geoff Miller and Nick Cooper.

lows: John Gill, banjo/ guitar/vocals; Dave Hibberd, Roger Wells, John Watson, drums; Nick Cooper, reeds, and Justina Underhay, bass.

In 1988 the Bath City recorded with Roy Castle in an I. T. V. Telethon appeal programme, "HOW WOULD YOU LIKE YOUR NOTES".

Bath City were a very active band and appeared at many different venues, (indoors and outdoors), fetes, launches and lunches, to name but a few. Their marching band attire was very impressive with 1920 style striped blazers and straw boaters. In their residencey at the Duke this formal attire gave way to a more casual and homely style. Step Whitehead however always managed some sartorial idiosyncratic item of dress. On one occasion at least a multi-coloured hand knitted woollen 'granny' scarf, more often the battered fedora, at rakish angle. Many Bog-enders however will remember his *piece de resistance*, the yellow wellies!

Pete Martin with other contributors

CRESCENT CITY STOMPERS

The band came into being after a conversation between the landlord of the Plume of Feathers, Hotwell Road, Ian (Flurge) Appleyard, Bernie Attridge and myself sometime in 1976. When the time came for the first gig the aforementioned musicians were not available. The eventual line-up was as follows: Nigel Hunt, trumpet; Derek Joynson, clarinet; Mike Cooper, trombone; John Macey, Bass; Roy Smith, drums and Jay Hawkins, followed by Dennis Harris and finally Wayne Chandler on banjo.

The Crescent City Stompers performed at the Plume of Feathers on Sundays and at the Mauritania on Monday nights. The Music style was New Orleans.

On one occasion when Gary Price was depping on clarinet for the Stompers he brought his pet crow with him. This crow would happily sit on the side of a pint glass. However, unnoticed by Gary during one of his solos, the bird crapped in Gary's glass. Neither the audience nor the band told Gary who finished the cider without comment. We did a number dedicated to the aforementioned bird called "Blackbird Blues," which entailed the creature perching on either the soloists instrument or body whilst playing the solo. All went well until the bird moved to the trombonist where the inevitable happened, the crow deposited it's unwanted material down the back of his shirt!

The band's demise came in 1978 with a change of music policy at the Plume of Feathers, great shame, the Sam Smiths at the Plume was excellent!

Mike Cooper

THE DON BURNELL QUARTET

This mainstream quartet was formed from a band which had played at the Coach and Horses in St Jude's, every Tuesday for about three years.

Don, in 1978, fixed a regular weekly session at the Bristol Bridge Inn, formerly the Postada, adjacent to the fruit market. After some time of well-attended and musically enjoyable sessions the management acquired a late licence. For some peculiar reason this did not result in bigger attendance's. In fact less people attended and not long after this the job came to an end and so did the quartet.

The highlight of the bands somewhat short life was a live broadcast from the pub on Radio Bristol's Jazz Tempo programme, compered by Jan Ridd.

The band's personnel were Don Burnell, clarinet / tenor sax; Ray Winter, piano; Dave Hibberd, drums/vocals; (Spud) Taylor, bass, replaced by Norman Cole.

Dave Hibberd.

KING STREET SEVEN

This band was formed at the suggestion of Alma Aniol, the then landlady of The Old Duke. There was then a vacant slot on Sunday evenings. Alma suggested that the band should include 'Duke' in its name. However, as The Duke Seven didn't sound quite right, they finally opted for the name King Street Seven.

There had been some doubt as to the year this band was first formed, but Roger Wells has produced the proof from one of his old diaries that it was 1973.

The original personnel were as follows: Ian (Flurge) Appleyard, trumpet; Chris Pearce, clarinet; Bob Reynolds, trombone; Dave Millman, piano; John Macey, bass; Roger Wells, drums, and Wayne Chandler on guitar/banjo.

The band developed quite a following helped by a few ladies at the Bog-end who would wave banners which declared that "CHRIS IS BLISS" and "WAYNE IS MAGIC" etc. Vocals were dispensed by Dave Millman, and also on occasions by a lorry driver from Norwich, John (nuts) Newell, who sang a few George Melly type numbers. John also arranged a few short tours of the Norwich area for the band. There was no band leader as such, but Flurge 'led' the band on stage.

When Bob Reynolds left Bristol to work elsewhere and Chris Pearce left to join the Bluenotes the band carried on for a few more months before disbanding.

The musical style of the band has been described as a Dixieland mix.

Wayne Chandler and Chris Pearce

THE 1980s

B G M TRIO

The 'B' stands for Brian Osborne the drummer, the 'G' is for Geoff Weldrake the double bass player, and the 'M' is for Mervyn Oxenham the pianist. The three have known each other for more than thirty years.

Brian started the band in 1988 at the request of the landlord of the Fleur de Lys at Pucklechurch who wanted more jazz at the pub. Brian was playing at the Fluer de Lys on Thursdays with the Phil Cotton Trio [Tony Bayliss on double bass]. B G M played there until moving to the Crown, Marshfield, in the early 1990s. About 1993 the trio moved to the Huntsman at Downend, at which venue they continue to play on Tuesday evenings.

Early on the band had a policy of inviting guests to play with them at regular intervals and this has continued to the present. There have been too many guest musicians to name them all, but to give a flavour of the variety a few are mentioned here: Frank Fennell, John Barton, Mike Wilkins, John Berry, saxes; Bruce Adams, trumpet; Mike Britton, Mike Watson, guitars; Arnold Kanarek, vibes; and recently, two young musicians, Osian Roberts, tenor sax and Andrew Coleman, trumpet, who was recently voted "Best Young Jazz Musician of the Year".

Geoff describes the musical style of the trio as Swinging Mainstream. They often play in Latin American rhythms. One of their supporters is a school governor who introduced the trio to his local primary school. This led to several occasions where the trio took their instruments to the school and

B G M at the Fleur-de-Leys, Pucklechurch, in the late 1980s. L to R: Geoff Weldrake, Brian Osborne and Mervyn Oxenham. The guest musician on this occasion is reed man, Frank Fennell.

friends who started a dance band at the Iron Acton Hall. They were called the Swing Commanders.

Geoff's double bass was too long for the car that the band was using, and so the neck had to stick out of an opened window. On a journey home after a gig the top of the double bass hit a high wall in Gaunts Earthcott and the scroll was snapped off. The main piece was retrieved immediately but some of the bits, (the nut), couldn't be found until the next day. The double bass was repaired and lasted another twenty years before being sold on.

After National Service there followed other dance bands. In the early 1960s Geoff was with the Denny Jordan Band in Trowbridge and then by 1974 he was with John

had musical sessions with the children from primary age upwards. These sessions were a great success, introducing the instruments and what they could do. This included the children rubbing tummies and patting heads at the same time to try and understand the complexities of drumming. There were many questions, mostly serious. One young girl asked Geoff, "How did you get it here?" (double bass.) Another question, not so serious, Geoff was asked, "How do you get that big 'guitar' under your chin?" Geoff's reply was, "It's easier if you keep your mouth shut!"

Geoff, in talking about the band, mentioned his own start in music, when in the early 1950s with two other lads they formed a harmonica band. This led eventually to his buying a double bass for £5 and taking it home on a bus wrapped in his overcoat. (So that's where Magritte got his idea from!) With this instrument he joined four other

Geoff and Mervyn performing at the Fleur-de-Leys in the late 1980s.

Critchinson's Trio. The trio consisted of Geoff, John and Reg Swain and they had a residency at the White Hart at Ford in "Jazz at the Icebox."

To return to the B G M - Brian says their claim to fame is to have played for Royalty, namely the Prince of Wales and the Duke of York, unfortunately they can't remember the names of the other pubs.

Compiled from information from Brian Osbourne and Geoff
Weldrake
Editor

THE DUKES OF SWING

I arrived in Bristol in early September 1979 from my Yorkshire home town of Bradford that had a modest jazz scene ranging from Trad to Free Form. It took me almost 48 hours to discover where the Old Duke was, and this renowned hostelry became my second home from then onwards. I soon began playing drums with a band that went on to become Six Piece Suite led by pianist Rod Coleman and trumpeter Bob Wade. One evening Bob and I were discussing Benny Goodman and he offered to lend me an LP of sextet recordings. I kept the record for an unreasonable length of time, returning it to Bob just before he left for, I believe, South Africa. The sound of the Benny Goodman Sextet knocked me out and I longed to play that kind of music. The majority of the bands I heard were playing in a broadly Dixieland manner and there were no bands in Bristol at that time playing that kind of swing style. I came to the conclusion that I would have to form a band of my own to satisfy my desires. The decision to do this was the easy bit - the hard work followed.

Which musicians were capable of playing that style and were available was my first problem. Clarinettist Nick Cooper was a natural choice with his superb Goodman like tone, melodic improvisation and knowledge of the idiom. I tackled him on my first gig with Henry's Bootblacks and he was interested. My next contact came at one of bass player 'Spud' Taylor's leaving gigs, just prior to his emigrating to Australia. I was playing, and up to the stage came a cloud of smoke followed by a pipe followed by a smartly dressed gentleman holding a guitar. This was the celebrated Jack Toogood.

Five minutes conversation convinced me that we were musically kindred spirits and we formed a close friendship that has continued to this day. Having said that, it took several hours of smooth talking to persuade this outstanding musician to join my embryo band! Jack had had a close association over many years with the much missed virtuoso Les Drake so he was the obvious choice to fill that chair. Les was much in demand, playing regularly with several outfits and persuading him to join an almost non-existent band with no work was not going to be easy. From memory the conversation when I asked him went something like this. Me, "Les, want a pint?" Les, "Yes please". Me, "Fancy joining my band?". Les, "Who's in it?". Me, "Jack Toogood". Les, "Count me in". Next came an offer of a gig from John Stone (who deserves a book of his own rather than mere mentions in this treatise) to play outside the Old Duke.

Besides those mentioned above I asked that excellent and much underrated bass player John Macey to do the gig, and he turned up. I also asked Bob Wade to do the gig, and he didn't turn up! The gig was in April 1983 and it went very well with another booking forthcoming from John Stone. Soon after the first gig I played at a pub called the Snooty Fox near Cheddar and met a vibraphone player with a never ending fund of jokes and funny stories, mostly concerning his own Jewish faith. Arnold Kanarek was as exciting to watch as to listen to and soon became a star of the band. Ex 'name bands' bass player Tony Bayliss eventually replaced John

Macey, and with myself on drums the line up was, for the time being, complete. All that remained was to find a name for this new enterprise. I filled reams of paper with probable names and discarded them all. I asked the band for their ideas. It took Arnold about ten seconds to come up with The Dukes of Swing.

Whilst our diaries were not overflowing with work we started to pick up odd nights at the Old Duke and some fairly regular work at the Civil Service Club in Horfield. Jerry Collins, an enthusiastic and hardworking supporter and booker for many Bristol bands ran the jazz nights there. He managed to persuade Radio Bristol to come and record the Dukes of Swing for a Jazz Tempo broadcast. We were all thrilled by the prospect and I for one believed it would lead to a considerable increase in bookings. I remember Les, possibly the most experienced member of the band, suffering an attack of nerves just before the recording and consuming numerous measures of Scotch. He needn't have worried. The recording went well and the band sounded very good. The Roger Bennett interviews were also successful and we received many favourable comments from those who caught the broadcast. I sat back and awaited the flow of bookings. The band didn't work again for six months.

The band's repertoire was mostly blatantly stolen from Benny Goodman, Artie Shaw and other Swing era bands. It amazed me how well the band played such tunes as "Seven Come Eleven", "A Smooth One", "Airmail Special", and "Oh Baby", without a single rehearsal throughout its entire being, a tribute to the high calibre of musicianship of all the players. By mutual consent we took Lionel Hampton's "Flyin' Home" as a closing theme tune and seldom did a gig without finishing with it.

The Dukes of Swing at the Beachcomber, Clevedon. L to R: Jack Toogood, guitar; Arnold Kanarek, vibes; John Watson, leader, drums; Mike Lindsay, bass, and Don Burnell, clarinet.

Work eventually began to appear. There were good and bad jobs, a few well paid and mostly (as ever) badly paid. Naturally, some notable ones come to mind including the legendary 'Wedding in Reading'! I met a Somerset man during a gig in Dusseldorf with the Severn Jazzmen. We chatted briefly during the intervals and he then disappeared. Some years later he came to one of the Dukes of Swing gigs at the Duke and asked if we would play for his wedding. He was certainly a young man of means and offered a substantial fee to play during the afternoon and evening together with a night in a hotel and free drinks! We naturally accepted and arrived on the appointed day at a beautiful Elizabethan hotel on the outskirts of Reading with a large marquee set up in the grounds for the post nuptial celebrations. The guests began to arrive from the registry office with somewhat gloomy expressions and it was obvious the 'bride' and 'groom' were no longer on speaking terms. It was explained that some important papers had not been produced and the registrar had refused to perform the wedding. Since there were several hundred guests it was decided that things should proceed as if the marriage had taken place, and we started to play. Things went well until the speeches that were obviously going to be difficult under the circumstances. The strained atmosphere was not improved during the 'groom's' speech when (after large quantities of alcohol) he concentrated on his friendship with me (the length of which could be measured in minutes) and the quality of the music, ignoring his 'wife' and her family and friends who made up the entire guest list. At

Glyn Howells at the piano. Glyn replaced the late Les Drake.

the end of the afternoon session most of the guests departed leaving only the 'bride's' close family to receive the multitude of friends expected at the evening celebrations. To show how well things were going my new found friend presented the band with our fee and a huge tip. We relaxed for a couple of hours and then got ready to play again. Meanwhile, the weather took an effect on proceedings and the heavens opened converting the steep narrow lane leading to the hotel into a muddy quagmire. Only a few guests made it to the

marquee but we played to this somewhat melancholy gathering. With an oversupply of drinks and a tense atmosphere the evening had only one inevitable ending. A fight started centred around my instantly ex-friend. Being true to our musical cause we stopped playing, packed up, looked for some spare bottles and went to bed. In the morning we found we were the only ones in the best hotel for miles around and we went home richer in finance and experience. I never did find out if the 'happy couple' eventually tied the knot.

Tragedy hit the band when we heard of the death of Les Drake under circumstances that remain unexplained. He was a wonderful and talented human being and is still missed by all that knew him. His replacement in the band was first the gifted Dave Lyon, then the ever-jovial Glyn Howells. Later still Nick left and the band changed slightly when that highly proficient pair Don Burnell and Geoff Nichols on clarinet and trumpet joined. The combination of a group of mostly professional musicians, trained to sight read music, together with the arranging and writing skills of Geoff and others opened new musical avenues. We started to play some of the more complex arrangements of the Artie Shaw Gramercy Five as well as more Goodman tunes and a couple of originals penned by Geoff. For some time we had been playing a regular alternate Tuesday night at the Duke and the band gelled into a precision swinging outfield with a considerable following.

Bands took turns in playing the 31st December at the Old Duke. It is traditionally the night when musicians command high fees and lousy gigs. I was unsure what to expect when New Year's Eve coincided with our Tuesday. With the exception of Tony Bayliss who had a prior engagement (and for whom the superb Clive Morton deputised) the entire band was present. The Dukes of Swing had never sounded better, the place was packed with an appreciative audience and the musicians unanimously voted it the best New Year's Eve gig any of us had ever played.

Unfortunately I had to leave the band in 1994 and it folded some time later. I still miss it desperately. I often said I felt privileged to play with such an eminent group of talented and professional musicians, and the feeling has never diminished. I also owe a debt of gratitude to the many musicians who deputised for the regular members, often at short notice and played the difficult arrangements so well. Recognition is also due to the wives and partners of the band members, including my own, who supported the group so well and in so many ways throughout it's existence.

It was a damn good band.

John Watson

FRAMPTON FOOTWARMERS

You could say that this band was formed in February 1986, although its origins were in the late Autumn of 1985. It all started because John Clutterbuck, the Rector of St Peter's, Frampton Cotterell, wanted to put on a variety performance featuring local people, to provide entertainment and also raise some funds for the church. At that time Susan Spedding was a member of the church social committee, and mentioned that her husband, Alan Spedding, used to play the trumpet and still owned an instrument.

When Susan returned home that evening and told Alan that he had been volunteered to produce a jazz band for the event, he was, to say the least, somewhat surprised. After all Alan had not played in earnest since he had left Liverpool for National Service some thirty years before, although he had always continued his interests in listening to jazz, mostly of the mid 1920s variety. His reaction was of the 'you cannot be serious' variety but 'she-who-most-be-obeyed' was firmly of the opinion that the die was cast, and prevarication would not be appropriate in the circumstances.

Clearly, a call must go out to find some local instrumentalists who might take part. Here the plot thickened, because Susan had a friend whose husband had played reeds some time before, and the ladies had already agreed that their husbands could do with a hobby to take their minds off of work. The friend's husband was David Cottam, who was keen to play his clarinet in the group, and with his help, a motley crew of jazz, rock and folk music volunteers was put together. Despite what might be called stylistic differences of interpretation in the band, the event duly took place in the nave of St Peter's Church, with the band attempting to achieve a Chicago jazz sound. Whether this was successful might be debatable, but the event caught the attention of the Minister of the Zion Chapel in Frampton Cotterell, who prevailed on the band to take part in a similar event a little later. A brave lady from the choir actually undertook to sing "Careless Love" with us, although she found the experience somewhat novel, and didn't find it easy to be heard above the racket we were making. Nevertheless the applause we received went to our heads, and Alan and David decided to find a local pub which would let us play for a nominal fee (called free beer).

The question of a name for the band had arisen and Alan remembered some of his early 78s and names like Rhythm Kings and Ramblers and of course the Eddie Condon Footwarmers band of the 1920s. The alliterative "Frampton Footwarmers" almost chose itself, although there was a short debate on Feetwarmers, but historicity was against this. The local pub turned out to be Daniels at Yate, which later became The Four Seasons and was then demolished to make way for a supermarket (Nothing to do with us, Guv!). The band opened there on Sunday evenings in February 1986, for which there was no fee, but a local enthusiast volunteered to be the can rusher to help us cover expenses. Expenses were incurred because, although we had acquired a piano player, there was no piano at the pub, so we hired a Fender-Rhodes electric piano. This was an electro mechanical contraption weighing more than one of us could carry, and it seemed to weigh more than two could carry by the end of the evening, because it had to be manhandled up and down a steep flight of stairs to the function room, involving some tight corners.

For some reason, which we could not understand, Yate was not ready for Chicago style jazz, even if we were interpreting the style a little freely, and so our 'season' was all too short.

However, some judicious chatting up led to a Sunday lunchtime gig in May '86 at the Plume of Feathers, Hotwells, at which the line up was Alan Spedding, trumpet; David Cottam, who moved on to double bass; Bill Firth, guitar; Alan Taylor, clarinet/tenor; Ron Baker, piano; Andy Youell, drums. Andy Leggett joined us for that gig on clarinet/baritone sax, to help with the Chicago sound. The first two personnel are still running the band, sharing the on stand leadership and publicity/management duties respectively.

Our first regular venue on Wednesdays from June 1986 to December of that year was The Quantocks, Weston-super-Mare, and also in December 1986 we began regular Fridays at Mr Popes in Bristol, which lasted until management policy changed in favour of pop groups in September 1990. During this period, David Bayliss joined us on slide trombone, which somewhat improved the authenticity of numbers like "Tiger Rag", "Farewell Blues" and "Tin Roof Blues". (Shades of the N.O.R.K.). Like many bands, we could not rely on finding playable pianos at venues, and we were each afraid of suffering a hernia carrying the 'portable' piano up and down flights of stairs. And so it came to pass that during 1987, pianist Ron left the band. Also because Andy appeared to be a rock drummer at heart, Roger Wells took up the drum chair on a regular basis until mid 1989, followed by the late, sadly missed, Tony McCarthy, until mid 1995, after which Brian Osborne joined us. Alan Taylor had, since 1986, been a stalwart member of the band, staying with us until he returned to London in January 1993, after which other clarinet/tenor players joined us, particular-

The Frampton Footwarmers at Yate Shopping Centre on National Jazz Day 1998. L to R: David Bayliss, William Firth, Alan Spedding, Brian Osborne, Robert Hughes, David Cottam and Mike Britton.

ly Robert Hughes, who is still a regular member. Depending on the type of gig we have included other musicians on a frequent basis, particularly Mike Britton, guitar, and during the various changes of personnel, when we were looking for replacements or deps we always found John Stone, the jazz loving landlord of the Old Duke to be a mine of useful information on the availability of jazz musicians. How times have changed!

There were several other venues which usually lasted for about a year or so, although one of the longest running at the time of writing, must be the King's Arms at Kingswood, which, it is difficult to realise, we first played at in 1990. This is due to the interest in jazz which the good-natured landlord, Roger, had always shown. Another long - standing venue has been Centre Parcs at Longleat, where we serenade the goldfish and ducks in addition to weekend guests. Over the years we have built up a good relationship with other organisations so that we have played quite a wide range of music at a variety of interesting places. These have ranged from repeat bookings to play jazz at various jazz festivals, regattas, balloon fiestas, opening supermarkets and shops, through to playing our style of music for dancing in five-star hotels from the south west through Bath to London.

We have also been fortunate enough to play on occasion with people like the trombonist, the late George Chisholm, the tenor player Tommy Whittle, and to have warmed up the audience for the Dutch Swing College band in a pre-festival concert in Bath. Our main criteria is that we play music we enjoy, which still relies more on the Chicago bands repetoire of the jazz age than on any other period. In response to overwhelming demand from our public, who regularly follow us to gigs on a unicycle, we have made three digitally recorded tapes, the most recent of which has also been produced on CD.

I feel sure that, like so many other jazz bands these days, we play because we enjoy it, and not for any expectations of being featured in the top ten. A few years ago jazz had larger audiences than generally exists now and it seems that these days we have often been hired to discourage some of the clientele which landlords prefer not to have, and to attract other types of people. However, it is a bit hard when we build up a strong attendance at a pub, and the landlord has to hire a bouncer to keep the crowd in order, and then sacks the band because he can't afford to pay a bouncer as well. It has happened, I assure you!

Alan Spedding

HOWLIN' WINDS

I formed Howlin' Winds Blues and Boogie Band to feature Dave Collett's talents almost exclusively in a blues and boogie context. Dave joined the Avon Cities about six months ahead of me in the early 1960s, and we worked together in the Dug Out, Park Street, often after completing gigs earlier in the evening! Our music commitments elsewhere were predictably jazz orientated and it was, at the time, pure indulgence for me to concentrate on Dave's blues/boogie piano style, and perhaps slightly angle it towards rocky.

Bass players at that time included Clive Morton, John Morton

The line-up for the first foreign gigs in Denmark and Paris. L to R: Chris Pope, Dave Collett, Paul Anstey and Andrew Barrett.

and Paul Anstey, the latter joining in time for our first foreign gigs in Denmark and Paris. Andrew Barrett was on guitar.

1992/98 saw the band undertake eight week long residences at the Slow-Club. Paris, and later at the Caveau Club on the South Bank. During this period Ted Brewster replaced Paul to complete the current line-up.

Private functions and club appearances (like the Avon's, notably and most frequently London's 100 club) provided a wide gig base for a, by then, very dancy programme. The current repertoire has gone full circle to include some contemporary jazz instrumentals featuring Andrew Barrett, but with anchorman Dave Collett firmly in evidence.

Our music is now drawn from a wide range of jazz and blues styles, including Leadbelly, Winton Marsalis, Van Morrison and Bob Seger. Add some original composition and gospel, and you have infectious dance music played by jazz musicians who enjoy playing the blues.

Chris Pope

PANAMA JAZZ BAND

The Panama Jazz Band was formed in 1989. I founded the band and recruited Lee Allen on clarinet and Dave Creech on trumpet. Initially we used a variety of rhythm players.

Our first gig was a lunchtime occasion at the Bush public house Totterdown. On the front line, Dave was the only experienced performer. I was playing trombone in public for the first time, although I had several years playing the sousaphone. This was Lee Allen's first ever public performance on the clarinet apart from occasional performances with the Bog end all Stars at the Old Duke! Dave Creech was so anxious

that we might not get through the gig that he arranged for Ron Brown, and I think Derek Joynson, to nonchalantly lean against the bar, with instruments in the boot of their cars perchance they were needed. A good deal of water has flowed under the bridge since then and we are now a well established Bristol band.

The band settled down with the following line-up: Dave Creech, trumpet; Lee Allen, clarinet; Bob Riddiford, bass, Dennis [Slim] Harris, banjo,and myself on trombone. After three years Dennis Harris left the band and in 1992 we were joined on banjo and guitar by John Currie from Swindon. John left the band in 1994 and was replaced by Wayne Chandler who stayed with us for two years. In 1996 Wayne left, and our present banjo and guitar player, Peter Holbrook, joined us. In the same year Dave Creech left the band and we recruited Tom Doughty from Bath.

Our regular venue for the past four or five years has been alternate Wednesdays at the Somerset House, Princess Victoria Street, Clifton, and for the last three years we have played the first Thursday in the month at the White Hart, Olveston, and the last Thursday at the White Swan, Swineford.

For the last three years we have an annual jaunt to Spain where we have taken two coach loads of jazz enthusiasts from the West Country.

Bob Coverdale

THE TITANIC TEAROOM QUARTET

Keith Warmington (Radio presenter), blues singer, harp player and old friend, then a teacher, phoned to offer me a gig. His teaching colleagues had hired the Tower Belle (ex London River bus) for a trip down the Avon Gorge on the 11th of September 1980. Could I organise a jazz quartet for them?

I called Charles Dalglish (cornet) with whom I had worked in the Midnight Follies Jazz Band (not to be confused with the Midnite Follies Orchestra), and John Gill of the Ken Scott Showband. Both said yes and with Robin A Wood (tuba); we duly assembled at Cumberland Basin for "Anchors Aweigh" at 6.30.

Roll Call:
Keith and teachers ?.....Present
Tower Belle?...............Present.
Water?... ....Absent!

Nick Grey who then owned the Tower Belle had misread the tide table and our maiden voyage had to be aborted.

A few phone calls and a quick drive later we reconvened in the function room of the Prince Rupert, Fairfax Street. The name "Titanic Tearoom Quartet" was the first that sprang to mind when I came to announce the band. For "Iceberg" read "Avon Mud"! The evening was deemed enough of a success to be repeated later the same month.

In the early days our repertoire was based largely on that of the "Midnight Follies" Jazz Band, Charles supplying us with his instantly recognisable chord charts. Each tune resembling the disembodied "Across" clues of a monster crossword designed to be read by shortsighted achoholics, in dim light, through smoke. A diet of Armstrong Hot Five and Fats Waller tunes plus a fair number of songs popularised by the Temperance Seven was on offer. Later on I provided a few of my own compositions which the chaps played with gratifying tollerance.

During 1986 Charles bowed out from the quartet under pressure of work and family commitments. For a time the Trumpet Chair .... yes we did play in the seated position more than most bands...... was occupied by the late Al Scott, Pete Martin or sometimes Graham Leavy, depending on the availability.

Since we all had other commitments musical or otherwise, a number of "deps" worked in the T T Q often enough to be regarded as honorary members. For example, when John was busy with the Bath City Jazz Band we used Reg Quantrill, Wayne Chandler, and (before he hung up his banjo-playing boots for good), Dick Wynn. Robin being a teacher, his place was often taken by Gus Gander, Henry Davies, Ken Fitzgerald or Tom Wittingham. Chris Pearce or Al Walker would dep for me. It was understood that if any of these came up with work for us, they would be included on the gig.

The quartet was sometimes augmented by an extra reed (Nic Cooper), Trombone (Step Whitehead), or more usually, drums (Tony McCarthy). I painted a cardboard insert for his bass drum amending the name to "Titanic Tearoom Quintet" complete with tasteful portrayal of a foundering ship. This logo also adorned the T T Q stationery and posters which had the added caption "GOES DOWN WELL." Incidentally the Titanic Society once booked us because of the name. We got to meet a survivor.

Apart from the Tower Belle we were not based at any single venue for more than a year or so. The band existed more to

The Quartet performing at a Graduation ceremony at St Matthias College, Fishponds. L to R: Bobby Mickleburgh, Andy Leggett, Tony McCarthy, and Reg Quantrill.

"Tiger Rag" and home we go.

We did this several times at Temple Meads; also at Bath, Gloucester, Swansea, Cardiff...Other memorable gigs included an enjoyable couple of days at the Henley Vintage Boat Regatta, The G W R s 150th birthday,and the chilly February day when we arrived to play at the Pedal Car Race on Durdham Downs precisely one month early. My mistake!

From mid '87 the trumpet parts duties were increasingly performed by the legendry Bob Mickleburgh, who merits a chapter all on his own. At the time he was still in the Temperance Seven and gigging locally with Henry's Bootblacks and the Gentlemen of Jazz.

Born on 26th September1920, he was taught to play by the Salvation Army. To my knowledge he worked with Jack Hilton, Roy Fox, Lou Stone, Sydney Lipton, Bert Ambrose, Billy Cotton, Stanley Black, Sid Phillips, Sid Milwood, Nat Gonnella.......I once made the mistake of announcing that he had worked with everybody but Dr Crock and his Crackpots. "I worked with Crock and his Crackpots" he growled. He appeared in Charlie Chaplins "A King in New York," and had spells running his own bands, the Bobcats, the Confederates and General Robert Mickelburgh's All British Orchestra.

Parting company with the Temperance seven in 1990 he had more time for us, and until I left for Germany in '96 he delighted me with his musicality and dry comments in that Norfolk draw.....

"Why does everybody play 'Georgia' too slow? You have all the dancers hangin' on one foot!"...

."Why do bands these days sound like a bass player accom-

provide lowish volume vintage jazz for weddings, birthdays, company events, fundraisers, vintage car rallies and the like.

We were booked repeatedly by Inter-City for locomotive naming ceremonies. This nearly always involved an early morning start, being on the platform half-an-hour before the arrival of the train in question, to provide a bit of jollity for the handful of windswept and pie-eyed dignitaries. The train pulled in. Steps complete with a frame and blue curtain worthy of a Punch and Judy show would be trundled up to the side of the loco. We blew a fanfare while the local mayor pulled a string, opening the little curtains to "reveal" the nameplate, which had of course been there all the time. The train would then pull out, without interrupting it's schedule, the passengers remaining bemused by - if not completely unaware of the - momentous goings-on up for'ard. A quick

panied by six blokes?"
If a tune went well, he'd come out with "Good enough for the dog with the Gramophone Company!"

Waking up in the back of the car in the wilds of Somerset, "What's that"? "Glastonbury Tor Bob." "Seems like a good place for it!" and back to sleep.

Arriving at a sleepy village we were to play in...."You could be famous here and no-one would know!"

Late one night driving home I offered him coffee in a Thermos . "Wonderful things Thermos Flasks " he said thoughtfully, "Mind you, bananas are good .....but TITS ARE BEST!" At the other end of the spectrum he resisted attempts to get him to play the Last Post, as it reminded him of days in the R A F when "I laid too many friends to rest."

Tragically the quartet had to do just that for one of it's own in Blagdon Parish Church. Robin Wood the tuba player died suddenly at 53. Larger than life he seemed made for the tuba, with a huge sense of fun. At an army camp one Christmas he rearranged the cardboard letters of a Christmas message on their strings to say something very rude and anatomical. When he played his eyebrows went up and down with his diaphragm. What a character, what a waste.

Subsequently the T T Q was driven along by the muscular bass playing of Justina Underhay. Bob's verdict..."She's better'n all the blokes." It remains to say that the T T Q continues to play aboard the Tower Belle, having covered many many miles in all weathers, with no incident more serious than a scrape on a lock wall or submerged car, or a tangle with the bottom when doing a thirteen - point turn with the river a bit low. Our thanks to Bristol Packet Company!

The Titanic Tearoom Quartet navigates on. All enquiries to John Gill.
.

Andy Leggett

VOCALS

"SOMEONE TO WATCH OVER ME" MOLLY COOMBES

Molly was about 18 when someone first asked her if she had ever thought about singing in a band. He had heard her singing with a small crowd of workmates while Molly was 'showing off' singing 'descant' as they called it then, more likely to be called 'harmony' or 'backing' now. Molly had a deep voice compared to the other girls, which many found amusing because she could never reach the high notes. This had led to some embarrassment for Molly when turns were taken round the class to sing and she was somewhat bemused that anyone should think she had a good voice suitable for singing with a band.

Several weeks later the same man was playing in an accordion band at a local school and requested that Molly come up and sing. She confesses to being extremely nervous, with her knees knocking louder than the drums but she did go up and sing the song which was at the top of the "Hit Parade" at the time, a song called "Change Partners", one of Kay Starr's hits. Other Kay Starr hits followed and Molly soon 'had the bug'. She started to enter singing contests at The Glen and Goram Fair at Blaise Castle and always managed to make the final three.

Next Molly went to Butlins with some friends, and entered more competitions there reaching the final heats of two competitions in one night for Photoplay Magazine and for the

Melody Maker vocalist of the year. This won Molly a free extra weeks holiday and entry to the next heat where she sang "Don't Blame Me", and won yet again. The next heat was in Birmingham - Molly was worried about travelling so far from home but she did go and of course she won again!

Molly performing at the Winter Gardens Pavilion, Weston-Super-Mare, in 1956.

While all this was going on Molly had been asked to sing at The Winter Gardens with the Ken Birch band every Wednesday and Saturday. Wednesdays were "Young Dancers" nights, which started at 7 o'clock and finished at 10. Lots of the RAF boys from Locking used to go there and it was always packed. Requests were handed up to the stage, written on scraps of paper for songs for 'someone special'. Favourites at the time were "It Only Hurts For a Little While"(Ruby Murray), "Only Fools Fall In Love" and "Ready, Willing and Able" which people liked for jiving. Dixieland numbers were popular until rock and roll started to take over, with "Rock Around the Clock". Molly also 'busked' with trad jazz numbers.

In the band at that time was Les Drake, piano; Maurice West, bass, and Arthur Wheeler, drums. Playing sax were Jack Wheeler, Tony Stone, Don Croft and Roy Harris. Colin Mushamp and Ken Birch played trumpet, with Ken leading. Bunny Millar also sang with the band. He was a great singer and character, and still is to this day. The band was the relief band for all the Big Bands which visited the Winter Gardens, such as Teddy Foster, Ivy Benson, Sid Phillips, Eric Delaney and many more. Those were the days! When the summer season ended they moved on to Pontins Holiday Camp at Sand Bay near Weston.

After that Molly was asked to sing with the Les Pursey band at the South Baths in Dean Lane, Bedminster. They used to put a false floor down over the pool and it got packed! The acoustics were great. Some of the bands from radio came to the South Baths when Molly and the Les Pursey band were there, The Kirchins being one - great stuff!

When Molly heard that the finals of the "Vocalist of the Year" contest would be held at the Royal Albert Hall in London she bought a strapless dress to wear. Molly took her husband-to-be, Ken, and her eldest brother with her for a night to remember. The judges were Jack Payne, Lita Rosa, and Eddie Calvert, Dave King, Frankie Vaughan and other 'Big Names'. Molly sang in front of the Joe Loss orchestra and came second, not bad for a little Shirehampton girl! Sponsors provided the prizes, and Molly was presented with a lovely powder compact, soap, talc, stockings and a cheque for £10 - a good sum in 1956. The song that she sang was "I'm in the Mood for Love". Other songs which Molly was singing at this time were "He's a Tramp" (the Peggy Lee version), "Hey There" and "Something's Gotta Give".

Then Molly was asked by Arthur Parkman to sing with his band at the Grand Hotel. Molly really enjoyed her time with this band - Arthur encouraged her to sing some lovely songs - "The Very Thought of You" was one of her favourites and also "You Make Me Feel so Young" and "Our Love is here to Stay". Molly did some radio broadcasts with Arthur backing on piano and vibes and trombone - a wonderful musician! She also started to do cabaret.

By this time Molly was married and started a family so the singing went on hold for a bit. While she produced her three sons Molly managed to fit in some cabaret as well as appearing on a daily news programme presented by Joseph Cooper on TWW, as it was then. She had been noticed on a Brian Michie talent show and was asked to do three appearances in one week.

For many years Molly worked for WD & HO Wills and sang for the Wills evening club as Jim, John and Molly. The keyboard accompaniment was provided by Jim Innols, a talented piano player - there seemed to be nothing he couldn't play. Molly's guests on those nights included Johnny Gordano, a great singer and impersonator, Robbie Moreno (what a character!), John Winters , Bristol's Frank Sinatra, and many more. Molly still meets people who remember those evenings and how good they were .The club still exists as the Luckwell Club, although it has been many years since Molly sang there.

For the last 15 years Molly has been singing with the New Parkway Showband. When she first started with them the male vocalist was Johnny Winters and Ray Bidwell also sang with them. Then along came a chap called Wayne Stanley, larger than life and a bit like Englebert Humperdinck - very dashing! Now the band has Roy Smith who has been with the band some years. He and Molly had worked together in the Ron Fowler Big Band. Roy is very popular - a happy person to have around.

Molly really enjoys singing with big bands - she says it gives her the chance to sing some wonderful songs including jazz, pops and ballads. Some of her favourite numbers are "If and When" (Shirley Bassey), "September Morn" (Neil Diamond), "In Your Eyes"(George Benson), and "I Need to be in Love" (The Carpenters). Molly especially likes singing ballads for the stories they tell and feels she has been very fortunate to have the chance to sing with so many different bands and fine musicians.

Later in her career Molly started singing jazz with the backing of what she considers to be some of the best musicians in Bristol,including the Dave Collett Trio. Although she has been singing for over 40 years in and around the Bristol area Molly confesses to still feeling very nervous singing in some places, and is still in awe of people who she feels are more talented than herself. However, as Molly says, "I always do my best". Those who are fortunate enough to have heard Molly will know just how good this is.

Molly has been threatening to retire for many years and perhaps one day she will, but "not yet " chorus her many fans, as they request once more for Molly to sing "Georgia" or "Someone to Watch Over Me".

Information from Molly Coombes
Editors

Dave has a real gospel feel to his playing, probably due to his admiration of Sister Rosita Tharpe and Mahalia Jackson with their accompanists.

The Avon Cities very generously provided this trio for the girls and also featured them at their club in the Green Room venue, King Street, this giving them instant experience to the thriving Bristol jazz scene.

I busied myself fixing gigs and broadcasts, and the girls performed for Radio Bristol's famous Jazz Tempo programme, BBC T.V., HTV and an enormous open air concert in Bath with the Chris Barber Band, (London's famous 100 club) and numerous other gigs. The girls were a sensation wherever

SHINE

Sometime after New Year's Day in 1978 I received a telephone call from an old friend, Pat Purchase, whom I'd known for many years. She rang to tell me that she had at last fulfilled a lifetime ambition to form a gospel group and would I come and hear them, and if interested, would I be available to manage them. Now Pat had a big reputation as a powerful class blues singer around Bristol and Bath, so I knew that it was bound to be a good sound. It took me a very short time to realise that this group of 3 girls (Pat, Kate McNab and Min Newman) really had an authentic feel for the music, a good repertoire and magnificent gospel sound, and above all was offering a completely different 'act' for the jazz scene. I accepted the position offered and set about finding a backing group and some musical exposure for the girls.

During my spell as manager for the Avon Cities I had built up a large network of contacts and venues including the press, radio and T.V. The Avon Cities Band at the time had, and still does, a fine rhythm section consisting of Dave Collett (piano), Chris Pope (drums) and Clive Morton (electric bass).

The group in full song at the Avon Cities Club in 1968. L to R: Kate McNabb, Pat Purchase and Min Newman.

they appeared, singing tunes such as "Step by Step", "Journey to the Sky", "Gone at Last", "Swing Low Sweet Chariot" and many others, with superb backing from the Dave Collett Trio. Pat sang with power and conviction, using

Shine shining. A photograph taken in 1978. L to R: Min Newman,
Pat Purchase and Kate McNabb.

her vast jazz experience. Kate was a strong partner in voice and personality and Min had a perfect sense of harmony, probably due to her previous experience in the folk scene.

Unfortunately success always brings problems - musical style differences, lack of their own backing group, reluctance to travel all over the country, and the desire to do something else. Sadly by mid 1978 the group was no more.

Pat virtually retired from the music scene to run her own business. Kate McNab joined the famous Sweet Substitute and Min Newman had a family and went to live in New Zealand.

Me? I'm still looking for musical talent wherever it might be.

Mike Bevan

SWEET SUBSTITUTE EARLY DAYS

The start of Sweet Substitute begins with Andy Leggett meeting Teriskemari Penfold at a party. Teri, in conversation with Andy said that she liked musical instruments, and the people that played them. She became aware of his collection within 24 hours. Andy later discovered that Teri could sing,keep time and pitch. This meeting was on the 5th April 1975, and by September that year they were married. In the meantime Andy had suggested to Teri that she contact Angie Masterson who Andy knew on the folk scene, and another singer Eiri Thrasher, also a folk singer. Angie was singing in a duo called Min and Ange and sometimes with a third girl called Jenny in a trio called Pussy. Andy's band was at the same gig as the trio and backed them on a couple of Boswell Sisters' numbers, "River Stay Away from my Door" and "Heebie Jeebies".

Andy suggested that the three of them should forget folk and concentrate on Boswell Sisters' numbers. The first get together was at Andy's house but he kept out of the way and so the first person to hear Sweet Substitute in song was a gas man who had called to do some repairs - lucky chap.

Andy got the band together again to back the new trio, temporarily called Fag Ash Lil. The backing band was Bill Brown, cornet player from San Francisco who was resident in Bristol, Bernie Newland, trombonist from London, a good friend of Andy's and his best man, Dave Griffiths, bass, Pete Hull, guitar and the late Tony Mc Carthy on drums. Occasionally Henry Davies would accompany on piano.

Fortnightly gigs were arranged by Andy at a place called Fanny's Bar, in Weston super Mare. On the first outing the girls did two numbers and subsequently four, then six and by the time that they were doing eight numbers news had got around about this new trio called Sweet Substitute. Roger Bennett gave the girls a chance to do a jazz tempo broadcast for Radio Bristol. The limited budget only allowed for a rhythm backing; Pete Hull and Andy on guitars and Dave Griffiths on bass. On the 15th January 1976 the Radio Bristol broadcast featuring Sweet Substitute was a Boswell Sisters repertoire with their characteristic changes of rhythm and key. They sang six numbers including "Cheek to Cheek", "Heebie Jeebies"," Fare Thee Well Annabel", "River Stay Away From My Door"and "Ford Engine Movements in my Hips".

A tape of this broadcast was sent to Kevin Daly, a producer with Argo, a subsidiary of Decca, who picked up on this exciting raw sound and suggested making a demo tape in the Yetminster Village Hall in Dorset where he was making an album with the Yetties. What was recorded has become known as the Yetminster tape. Sweet Substitute were backed by the whole band (see above for personnel). The outcome was that the Girls passed the audition - but the band didn't. Andy relates that the vocal arrangements at this time were carefully worked out whereas the band's arrangements didn't get such close attention.

Several months passed by and they were notified that studio sessions were booked and that Keith Nichols and Alan Cohen were engaged to write band arrangements around Andy's vocal arrangements. Incidentally, Keith and Alan had just finished recording an album with Bing Crosby. Everything was ready to go when Eiri suddenly and regretfully announced that her husband had to move to a new job and that she would be leaving the group. Frantically they set about auditioning for a new singer and after many aspirants that for various reasons didn't measure up to the musical demands, a singer known as Sammi Brown got the job. Sammi, born Christine Price of the very musical Price family had sisters who sang and brother Gary, the amazing busker who set fire to his hat when performing and at one time had a pet crow. Chris really fitted the group, had a really husky voice and immediately the group sounded a lot more like the Boswell Sisters.

The date came for the first recording session. The group arrived in the transit van at Decca No.4 studio, Tollington Park, Finsbury, and were astonished to find 27 musicians lined up to accompany the girls; this is where Kevin Daly coined the name for this backing group The Midnite Follies Orchestra for the tracks which Alan Cohen arranged with strings. On one track Kevin had a Compton theatre organ played by Ronald Curtis which was dubbed in later. It came to light later that Ronald Curtis was Kevin's cousin, so a bit of nepotism going on there. "Heebie Jeebies" was recorded with Keith Nichols on piano only, also a small group accompanied the girls on some numbers.The line-up was; Brian Daly and Vic Flick, guitars, (the latter played on the Coronation Street signature tune and the 007 theme); Mo Morris, violin; Roy Babbington, bass, and Trevor Tompkins, drums.

A little note here about the voices-Teri had the highest voice and usually took the top line, middle harmony was Angie and Chris the bottom line.

Kevin and Andy were in the booth listening and while the orchestra, augmented with strings, were playing, Kevin was rubbing his hands together and saying, "THIS IS COSTING MONEY!" It was the biggest budget he had been let loose on at that time. Kevin was a very heavy smoker and unfortunately is dead now, a great loss having been a great collector of '78' records with extensive musical background knowledge.He wrote several books and many sleeve notes for L P's.

The first Decca Sweet Substitute album "Something Special", No. D1 SKL 5270, came out in 1977,and became Radio 2 album of the week and shortly afterwards Sweet Substitute were asked to do "Friday Night is Music Night", live from the Festival Hall, with Geoff Love and the Radio Orchestra.
Decca insisted that Sweet Substitute had a manager The first one was Dave Curtis who was then manager of the Pasadena Roof Orchestra, and still is. He organized a Sweet Substitute tour with the PRO, which included a trip to Berlin that was very exciting, as the 'Wall' was still up at the time. Venues included the Berlin Philharmonic Hall, and on the same tour the Sonesta Hotel in Amsterdam. The tour continued in the UK with the Festival Theatre in Chichester followed by a flight to Hamburg for a recording with Keith Nichols who was the musical director. The album is on the Transatlantic Label No:0064.010, Kevin Daly being the producer.

Sweet Substitute were now appearing on T.V. in Europe and the U.K. In 1977 "Jazz on the Quay", staged between The Old Duke and The Llandogger Trow featured The Avon Cities with an appearance of Sweet Substitute backed by a quartet.The line-up was Henry Davies, piano; Andy Leggett, clarinet and guitar; Bernie Attridge, bass, and Gordon Smith, drums. The girls arrived in style for their spot (a Bentley). Unfortunately Henry had been taken ill but Keith Nichols was on hand to save the situation!

The BBC commissoned a half-hour show recorded at the Fulcrum Theatre, Slough. The backing band included Digby Fairweather on cornet, Bill Skeat, Mel Thorpe and Andy on Saxes and Pete York on drums. About this time there were two shows for HTV "Christmas Sweet", and just after a tour with the Syd Lawrence Orchestra, a show called "Sweet and Stately". This was to be shot at Dyrham House with such scenes as "Your Feet's Too Big" in the Boot Room surrounded by shoes and other props. Due to a technicians dispute the whole thing was done in the studio with no staging, and a very sparse affair it turned out to be!

Sweet Substitute also did T.V. shows in Belgium, at the American Theatre in Brussels, and a T.V. show in Stockholm. Sweet Substitute were on a five year contract to Decca and having released the first record in 1977 they carried on recording and did enough numbers for four more albums, but

Publicity photograph of Sweet Substitute. L to R: Angie Masterson, Teri Leggett and Sammi Brown (Christine Price). Photograph, copyright Decca Music Group.

they were never issued. However, a few singles were released. Decca tried to pursuade the girls to do rock and roll material, and it was only by stout persistence that none were included in the first L.P. Decca might have preferred to be marketing ABBA.

During the time the albums were not being released, Sweet Substitute were less in demand for live work. Andy felt that if they wanted pop material Sweet Substitute should at least write their own. So they did a single "A Musical Chistmas

Card." It got a lot of airplay with Pete Murray, Jimmy Young and Terry Wogan - it didn't hit the shops until February!

At this point Andy started to arrange much of the instrumental as well as the vocal parts, as Sweet Substitute were now performing with various orchestras including some in the BBC. As no one fell about laughing at the results of these arrangements he felt encouraged to persist. Alun Ainsworth was also commissioned to do some arrangements: all these are in the BBC vaults going to waste. Who will buy it up and put it out as "Sweet Substitute, The Lost Years?"

About this time Chris got herself a new boyfriend and decided her future lay in looking after his handful of children. Before she left, Decca brought out a single "We Just Couldn't Say Goodbye" backed by a band including Digby Fairweather, cornet; Pete Strange, trombone; Randy Colville, clarinet; Keith Nichols, piano, and Andy on guitar.

Enter Kate McNab. The group now sounded less like the Boswell Sisters and more like The Andrews Sisters. In 1980 Sweet Substitute played for a month in Zurich where it was suggested that Andy arrange an Andrews Sisters medley. The girls were frequently engaged for Radio 2 Shows, broadcast from the Paris Studios, (where the Goon Shows were recorded). Shows they appeared in included, Peter Goodright, Frankie Howard, and Arthur Askey Shows. Kate's ability as a singer had already been well known to the group but it was impressive how quickly she picked up the repertoire.

When Sweet Substitute finally came out of contract with Decca they recorded for Alan Bates of Black Lion Records. The L.P. No: INT 161.539, and Tape No: INT 461.539 were eventually issued on a German label called AVES in 1981. This recording included three of Andy's own compositions, "Tiger Blues", "Sleepy Suzie" and "Dear Mr Berkeley". Two of the numbers were backed by the Chris Barber Band, two numbers by Digby Fairweather and Friends and other tracks with a mix from unaccompanied voices to a sixteen piece orchestra. Kenny Baker and Danny Moss were two of the luminaries present in a very impressive line up of musicians.

The girls toured with Keith Smith's Hefty Jazz, notably on the "Stardust Road " tour with Georgie Fame, featuring Hoagy Carmichael songs. Also they teamed up with Ralph Laing and Groove Juice Special, and eventually with Kit Morgan and small group backing. However, Sweet Substitute's later performances with the above mentioned bands is worthy of a more detailed account, but that's another story. Teri, eventually left Sweet Substitute to be replaced by Suzi Knowler. Angie Masterson died on the 20th February 1999. She was a pivotal member of the group, not only a superb singer, dancer and guitarist but a lovely person who will be greatly missed.

Editor's interview with Andy Leggett

COMEDY BANDS

THE ALLIGATOR JUG THUMPERS

This is how I heard it.

Around 1966, Adge Cutler confided his plans to form a band called the Wurzels to Cliff Brown, formerly drummer with Acker's Chew Valley Jazz Band. Cliff came away with the impression that he was to go ahead and find musicians and start rehearsals.

By the time he became aware that the Wurzels were already in existence, he had been joined by Barry Back on guitar and Quentin Williams on kazoo, plus assorted hardware, both singing as well.

Adge was good enough to offer the trio the job of closing the first half of his "Scrumpy and Western" shows at the Colston Hall and elsewhere. This was where I first heard them in 1967. I already knew Barry and his close friend Fred Wedlock, compere of these shows, through the Troubadour Folk Club in Clifton, where I had been playing guitar and tin whistle with Flanagan's Folk Four.

The Alligators produced a bouncy mix of jazz tunes and self-penned numbers: Barry's "Blues Crazy Baby", Q's "Don't Smile At Me" and "Jug Thumping Morons From Home", and Cliff's "Motorway Song".

Apart from the guitar and kazoos, much of the gear was home made, starting with the uniforms. Milkmens' jackets dyed red with tape sewn round the edges, and hand embroidered alligator-rampant badges on the vest pockets.

Cliff, a noted cartoonist, and an animator with the West of England Film Unit, was an indefatigable creator of joke instruments. In his hands a fly-spray became the 'Flit-a-flute'. His wife Rhoda grew indignant when their ornate Indian brass vase, standing waist-high with a wide mouth at the top was one day perforated to receive a mouthpiece at the lower end. This became the 'Karma-Sutraphone'. A kazoo was grafted onto the painted intestines of a table gramophone to create the 'Thunderbox'.

Cliff himself performed on the 'Stud-Box', (a loud washboard-substitute made of plywood and furniture tacks, played with four fingers of each hand inserted into empty cartridge cases); he also played the 'jug'. This was a glass beer or cider flagon decorated by Rhoda, with oil paints using a gramophone turntable like a potter's wheel.

Barry's guitar style owed more to skiffle than to Segovia. Ordinary plectrums would escape his grasp in seconds, so he chose to thrash away with a bluegrass-type thumb-pick. He played open chords and relied on a capo to change key. This, in tandem with Cliff's stud-box produced a rhythm like primitive agricultural machinery, so it's lucky he had a loud voice too.He had the same trouble with kazoo's as with plectrums. The only one which wouldn't keep popping out was the disc-shaped 'Humazoo', which the teeth could clamp on to. Conversations tended to continue, 'Clangers' style, despite this impediment.

Q. Williams tired of the travelling, and a replacement was sought. I was invited to a musical party at Cliff's Timsbury Bottom Studios, not realising that it was an audition, which I was then told I'd passed. I played only guitar at the time, having sold the clarinet I'd played in school and university jazz bands.

Q gave me a crash-course in the repertoire. We played on more Adge Cutler concerts, appeared at the Keynsham Donkey Derby and, after Barry had been replaced by Alun Ashworth Jones (inventor and manufacturer of the "Ashworth" guitar pick-up), embarked on a tour of Devon folk-clubs. Cliff complained that the folk music was "too doomy" and ultimately went on to found the Alligator Jazz Band, (later to include Q and me).

In the meantime, I teamed up with Barry Back once again, and with Dave Creech and John Turner formed the Pigsty Hill Light Orchestra, reviving some of the Jug Thumper's repertoire.

But that's another story.

Andy Leggett

THE PIGSTY HILL LIGHT ORCHESTRA

The band was formed to play at the Troubadour club Clifton after Fred Wedlock's New Year party 1968. All the original band members came from various well-known groups, Dave Creech from the Elastic Band, Barry Back and Andy Leggett from the Alligator Jug Thumpers and John Turner from the Downsiders.

They employed a variety of unusual and unorthodox objects as instruments, and the style of music was 20s and 30s Jazz and Blues. The band produced a unique and original sound

The band in 'regimental' attire. L to R, back row: Barry Back, Dave Creech and John Turner. Foreground: Andy Leggett, in the late 60s photograph.

from the unlikely assortment of instruments, jugs, plumbing pipes, funnels, hot water bottles and toilet ballcocks etc.

All this mixed with a lot of enjoyable comedy and good humour got them voted the band "most likely to succeed" by the Melody Maker following the album PHLOP! released in 1970.

In 1970 John Turner left the 'piggies' to work on other musical projects and the band was joined by Wild Bill Cole, a fine bass player whose talents were demonstrated on their next album "Piggery Jokery" recorded in Redruth in Cornwall in 1973.

Dave recalls a time when Barry was still working for H T V in Cardiff, when a gig in Kings Lynn, Norfolk, had been cancelled at the last minute. The rest of the Pigs who were in Leeds tried to let Barry know by all possible means.(no mobile phones then folks)! Barry could not be contacted and drove all across southern England to find out the gig wasn't on. He then drove back to Cardiff for an early morning start!

Whilst playing Stalybridge, (Lancashire) the band had been unable to book accomodation and asked the fans at the gig if they knew of anywhere they could stay. A punter offered beds for the night and invited them back to his pub, (he was the landlord). When they arrived about half past midnight the place was packed and jumping.........everyone there was a copper! They had to play all over again and didn't get their heads down until about 4am.

Later in 1973 Barry Back called it a day and was replaced by Jon Hays, also known as 'Wash', short for washboard. During the next eighteen months the band experienced many changes, notably the departure of Andy Leggett. During this period, through the doors of "Piggy Towers", came Dave Paskett, Pat Small, Henry Davies, Ritchie Gould, two fine guitarists Robert Greenfield and Chris Newman, and an occasional guest, a bewildered Diz Disley. All these musicians featured on the next album "The Pigsty Hill Light Orchestra 1976".

Considering the quite frequent changes in the line up the band still had a strong following. However, in 1979, after a successful ten years in both the U.K. and Europe the PHLO decided it was time to retire.

In 1988 Barry Back was asked to reform the PHLO for a one off performance at the Village Pump Festival at Trowbridge. On the bill that weekend were Dave Creech, Andy Leggett, Bill Cole, Jon Hays and Barry Back, almost the original team.

The band was reborn and returned to tour extensively, picking up ex- piggie Pat Small on the way, and Hannah Wedlock, vocalist, who added a whole new dimension to Piggie Music. The revival was expressed in the 1991 album "Back On The Road Again".

The end of 1991 saw further changes with Jim Reynolds and Dave Griffiths joining the band, and in 1992 a "Musical History" album was issued combining a selection of tracks from 1968 to 1992.

Barry was the instigator and the enthusiast for the re-forming of the Pigs and his sudden and untimely death in 1992 dealt a devastating blow to the rest of the group, and his loss meant that the joy of performing had disappeared. The professionalism of the band was highlighted in that they went on to honour all their commitments, but once again it was time to call it a day.

During the life of the Pigs they toured extensively in the U K and Europe: Ireland, Belgium, Holland, Germany, France, Switzerland, Denmark and Luxembourg, (the latter they can't remember whether they played in, or just passed through),all were hosts to Bristol's own brand of musical madness!

Compiled from information supplied by Dave Creech
Editor

VENUES

BRISTOL JAZZ CLUB

Joe Brickell, the Bath trumpeter, wrote a few notes about the Bristol Jazz Club shortly before his death in October 1998.

The working life of the club ran from 1949-1951, meeting on Thursday evenings at their 'headquarters', the Provident Ballroom, Prewett Street, Redcliffe.

The President of the club was Steve Race, who was to become a Radio and T.V. musical presenter. One member of the committee was Randolph Sutton, the much loved and famous music hall artiste. He was well-known for his rendering of "On Mother Kelly's Doorstep", his signature tune for many years (See Severn Jazzmen). One of the club's functions was the operation of a Record Exchange.

From the examination of an original membership card the rules would appear today to have been somewhat draconian,although interestingly enough the minimum age for membership was only 14 years.

Joe mentions the musicians who were the stalwarts of the club: On piano; Glyn Wilcox, Den Smith, Len Cook, Mervyn Oxenham and Jimmy Dunsford. On guitar; Frank Evans, Jack Toogood, Mike Watson and G. N. Clemo. On drums; Ray Stevens, Pete Simmonite, Johnny Cox and Roy Phillips. On bass; Sid Uppington, Maurice Everson, Mark Cottle, Les

Jenkins and Ray Smith.   On alto-sax; Ivor Smith. On tenor sax; (Lucky) Lovell. On clarinet; Art Hallet and Pete Conibear. On trumpet; Granger Rock. Vocalist; Pam Coster. Glyn Wilcox (piano) also played trombone. All sessions were staged and compered by guitarist Les Britton.

The club was a popular venue for miles around, the 11. pm. train from Temple Meads being crowded with Bath teenage club members.

In January 1950 Joe Brickell and Glyn Wilcox were among musicians who took part in a memorable Bristol Jazz Club 'Riverboat Shuffle'.

Dave Hibberd

THE OLD DUKE

The Beginning - According to Alice

One day in 1965 Trevor Bricker came up to me and said, "Hey man, we've found this pub down town where they'll let us have a blow! Come on down on Sunday morning." So Clive and I donned our bicycle clips, carefully placed cornet and banjo in the panniers and duly pedalled the tandem down to The Old Duke in King Street where there were assembled a dedicated collection of New Orleans jazzers, all wound up and ready to play. My memory is not up to remembering all the musicians on that very first session but I know Pete Child was on trombone and Trevor on clarinet.

Clive and I didn't miss a Sunday morning after that for years, either sitting in or not, depending on how many musicians turned up. As the crowd started to build up someone suggested that perhaps the landlord would give us free drinks (money was never discussed in those days!) - and that was decided upon, until it was discovered how much we could all

put aside in one session, so it was then rationed to one pint on the way in and one in the interval, this to be handed to the band on a tray just in case anyone cheated.

In 1966 Clive joined The Okeh Rhythm Kings led by pianist Gerry Bath and on the 1 April 1967 they rented the upstairs room and started a jazz club. Mike Edkins who managed the band and his wife Sheila manned the door charging 2/6d admission.

The other members of the band were Clive Taylor, clarinet; Pete Kendall, trombone; Robin Wood, banjo; Gerry Gittens, drums, and Jed Collard, - sousaphone. Jed's wife Hazel was the vocalist and I used to sit in on banjo on most Saturday evenings.

At one time we used to have around 150 people enjoying our classic jazz style and dancing around. Unfortunately, a halt was called to the dancing when it was noticed that the front wall was gradually moving outwards towards the Llandogger. Each week the gap between my chair and the street below seemed to get larger. They hung a tarpaulin across the wall to hide it, but I must say it didn't improve my nerves much. Eventually, after a couple of months of dangerous banjo playing, scaffolding was erected and the building screwed back together. Whew, was I glad!

Every now and again guest bands were booked to appear alongside us. I remember the Zenith Hot Stompers from Birmingham, the Frog Island from the London area and the wonderful Red Onions from Australia.

The Okeh's had a few personnel changes over the years. When Robin Wood left I took over on banjo. Jim Scadding replaced Pete Kendall on trombone and Bob Phillips replaced Gerry Gittens on drums. Now this is where it became a family band! Follow this! Jed Collard's wife Hazel sang - she was Jim's cousin. Jim's wife sister was married to the drummer and I was married to Clive. OK?

Meanwhile, downstairs every Saturday evening, things were

also swinging with Brian 'Spud' Taylor on piano. He played there until 1974, when unfortunately the Okeh's finally split up in 1972, when we all went our separate ways and joined other bands.

Clive and I joined the Panama Jazz Band led by Robin Wood the pianist, not the same Robin Wood who played banjo with the Okeh's. Sadly neither of these lovely men are with us today. We used to play every Monday evening at The George and Railway near Temple Meads.

Following a few personality clashes between myself and another member of the band, involving a history book and a long string of red knitting (well, that's another story!) I decided to leave and form a band of my own and so, Alice's Wonderland Band came into being.

In 1978 we returned to the Old Duke with the following line-up: Clive, cornet; Alan Taylor, clarinet/sax; Bob Mickleburgh, trombone; Brian Walker, sousaphone; Robin Wood, piano; Gordon Smith, drums, and myself on banjo. Tragically, Gordon was killed in a car accident in 1980 and we found it very difficult to replace him, especially as he had such a wonderful personality.

We originally played on Mondays, then Saturdays and, eventually alternate Tuesday evenings up until the 'Fall of the Empire.' John Stone's departure and subsequent changes at the Old Duke.

The personnel of our band when we left the Duke was Clive, cornet; Andy Leggett, clarinet/saxes; Tom Whittingham,(our son) trombone/washboard etc; John Massey, double bass, and myself on banjo.

I hope my memories of the beginning of jazz at the Duke have been fairly accurate, but I am sure someone will make a few corrections. Facts and dates would be most welcome.

Jill Whittingham

THE OLD DUKE

THE GOLDEN BOWLER

On Monday 5th June 1978 John and Mauveen Stone took over the Old Duke Public House in King Street, Bristol. They had been told that jazz bands used to play there regularly, but that had stopped some years previously. John, being an ex Royal Marine Bandmaster couldn't wait to get things going again. He made enquiries about bands in the area, and slowly but surely got in touch with them and arranged for them to play on different nights of the week, the high spot being Sunday Lunch times.

In 1980 John started a Jazz Festival at the Duke which lasted

The 'Bog End' of the Old Duke with, L to R: John Stone (landlord), Ian (Flurge) Appleyard, (Doc) Cheatham, Norman Hill and Mike Cocks; A fanfare of trumpeters.

88

for seven days during the month of August. Over the years this became a world - wide known Festival. After much deliberation it was decided to run it over the three days of the August Bank holiday. The jazz started outside the pub on a specially erected stage at midday until 11pm. It was a tremendous success. The regular bands who played every week at the Duke had their special slots and there were guest bands and solo artists from all over the country, and sometimes from abroad to take the stage.

John and Mauveen also arranged a two-week trip to New Orleans for some 50 of the regular customers. It was a won-

John Stone, sporting his New Orleans Golden Bowler at the Old Duke, saying farewell to two punters (Tess Green and John Griffiths) on the last night of his residency, 5th January 1995.

derful visit to the birthplace of our much loved Jazz. John and Mauveen ran the Duke for some 16 years, and it never lost its popularity as one of, if not the best, jazz venues in the country. John could be seen at the end of the evening donning his 'Golden Bowler' (from New Orleans) taking up his trumpet and playing "The Saints" or something like it, then taking up his baton and conducting a sing-song of the 'Bog Enders'. It was with much sadness that on January 5th 1995 that John and Mauveen had to leave the Duke because of a change in Brewery policy. The Duke only has Jazz a couple of times a

week now, but it is hoped that it will still carry on and who knows, the tables could be turned, and it becomes once again the 'gig' to play at.

Mauveen Stone

THE GRANARY 1968-1978

It doesn't seem that long ago but the year it all happened was 1968!

I was manager of the Avon Cities Jazz Band at the time and jazz was doing quite well, both in Bristol and the rest of the country, with gigs in clubs, pubs and barbecues - local boy Adge Cutler was top of the open air attractions and the Avons were playing at Blackboy Hill in an extraordinary place called the Moulin Rouge which featured turn of the century Parisian Night Club décor complete with cubicles.

During 1968 the band was forced out of the Moulin Rouge which had rapidly become a meeting place for a non jazz clientele .... But as they say when one door shuts, etc .....

The door that opened was that of a completely new venue for Bristol - an old derelict grain store built in Bristol Byzantine style called the Old Granary, situated on Welsh Back behind the Llandoger Trow pub in the now famous King Street area. My involvement started in early September 1968 when Ted Cowell and David Bilk (Acker's Brother) appeared at my front door (to my surprise) and requested a meeting. Ted is a very old friend of mine, a great jazz enthusiast and an expert at the conversion and re-styling of property. In fact he was working for the Bilk organisation doing just this sort of thing. Dave Bilk managed Acker's business investments and looked after his Capricorn Club in London.

Mike Bevan, second left, greeting Jimmy Rushing (ex Count Basie singer),on the American's visit to Bristol.

What they had come to talk about was the fact that they were going to lease this incredible building from the Council and convert it into a seven day a week jazz club. This included a restaurant on three of the seven floors of this enormous building and would I be interested in being the manager? Their plans were grandiose and many famous international jazz names were bandied about and I was filled with enthusiasm - after all wasn't this what Bristol needed? One mustn't forget that there were no permanent jazz venues in the city - The Old Duke was just another King Street pub along with the Naval Volunteer and Llandoger , none of which had a serious musical policy.

I wrestled with the decision for about three weeks and finally decided against the position offered, but they persuaded me to help in the organisation and running of the club, and as I had an agent's ticket, to book all the local jazz bands which were required to support the main national attractions. This suited me very well as promotion was looming in my day job!

Work started in earnest on the building which had been empty for about 25 years. Many of the top floors were perforated and open to the elements and quite unusable, but the ground 1st and 2nd floors were sound and could be easily turned into a rather spectacular jazz club. The upper floor was partially cut away so that jazzers could sit upstairs and view the various antics of the dancers below.

The Bar was the longest in Bristol, with beer pumped up from the cellar room 30 ft below. The restaurant was of the bistro type and sported a glamorous Jamaican lady chef (who did the best and cheapest steaks in town). There was also a small intimate bar on the upper floor. The upper floor also had something completely new to Bristol, a room devoted entirely to the manipulation of the house public address system and disc playing equipment, plus the ability to control the stage lighting and effects, which were later to include light shows. The sound system which was enormous was designed to suit this large building by jazz clarinettist Sandy Brown, who was a BBC acoustics engineer between gigs.

The policy of the club was to bring together all the jazz punters and give them the absolute best of everything at a moderate price. All Bristol waited with anticipation for the grand opening due in October 1968.

The opening day arrived on Tuesday, 8 October, with music supplied by the Avon Cities Jazz Band, and everybody with the slightest connection with the scene was there. It was fantastic, the level of happiness only rivalled by the happy crowds on the City Centre on V.E. Day. The band played,

Maynard Ferguson and his band performing at the Granary.

Kenny Ball, Chris Barber, Humphrey Lyttelton, Monty Sunshine, Ken Colyer, Terry Lightfoot, Sandy Brown, Alex Welsh, and their bands provided wonderful evenings at this, by now trendy jazz venue.

International jazz stars such as Maynard Ferguson, Ruby Braft, Red Norvo, Teddy Wilson, Muddy Waters, Joe Harriott, George Wein, all appeared at various times. Stars such as Paca Pena, John Mayer, Long John Baldry, Alan Price and Georgie Fame helped fill the jazz and R&B fringe requirements.

The success of the Granary Club soon caught the attention of the media - leading national newspapers called it the most successful jazz club in Europe, more than rivalling those in London. HTV filmed in the place and Humphry Lyttelton compered a live Jazz Club Broadcast from there in 1969, featuring the Avons and Bluenotes plus the John Critchinson trio with Sammi Brown - critics noted the piano sounded like something Mrs Mills would have rejected and Roger Bennett was voted musician of the evening - but still a good time was had by all.

celebrities abounded and the booze was free! The Granary was launched in style.

The jazz policy adopted by the parent company was to provide named British jazz bands, international jazz names and the best of local jazz. Owner Acker Bilk was the first name band to appear and that was on 10 October - with the band resplendent in their current uniform of bowler hats, striped waistcoats, shirts and black pants. Friday nights were reserved for the Avon Cities and Monday's featured folk music for a time. The Blue Notes who had lost their famous Ship venue in Redcliffe Hill moved into the Wednesday slot, and the New Chicagoans, Henry's Bookblacks, the Okeh Rhythm Kings and many others filled out the spaces between the Big Names.

The carefree manager of the club was a smart young chap called Rod Dowles who had been bar manager at Acker's Capricorn drinking club in London - he really enjoyed his role but secretly he missed the London scene and after a period he disappeared, and the club was managed by a group which included myself (still on a part-time basis).

To run a seven day a week jazz oriented club in the provinces successfully is a very difficult task, and the management felt they had to introduce musical variety. Monday nights (always quiet) were considered for a different sound. Around about this time Mike Tobin and Al Read were running a very successful Rock/Pop scene in a basement club in Park Row known as the Dugout, and it had become too small for the large numbers attending. An approach was made and they literally transferred their activities to the Granary on Mondays, and later to Thursdays as well. The Bluesy / pop sound started to attract very large crowds and the phsycadelic atmosphere created by bands such as Genesis, Status Quo and Dire Straits, plus a light show became one of Bristol's places to be.

Sadly the support for live jazz diminished, the jazzers seemed uncomfortable in an atmosphere of film projectors, disco lighting and the paraphernalia associated with large rock bands - the piano regrettably never recovered!

The Granary suffered a series of financial crises which seemed extraordinary when the placed was jammed to capacity with eager dancers and drinkers. There were several management changes - a bankruptcy and a set of new owners, but unfortunately The Old Granary ceased trading in 1978.

Looking back on the jazz years I don't think we realised what a fantastic club it was - I've been in many jazz venues around the world and I think The Old Granary was the best.

Let's hope that jazz will survive, and eventually aspire to it's own purpose built home again some day.

Mike Bevan

KING STREET

Since the late 1960s jazz has been a particular feature of King Street, and with the start of the summer Jazz Festivals by John Stone, landlord of The Old Duke in 1980, the street could itself be called a venue.

At theWelsh Back end of the of the street on the quay was moored a converted Lightship which hosted some jazz gigs during the 1980s. Just around the corner the Granary opened in 1968 as a jazz club venue for local, national and international bands and performers. (see the Granary, page 86).

The Old Duke had it's first jazz gigs in 1967 with the Okeh Rhythm Kings playing upstairs. (see Okeh Rhythm Kings, page 48). The first Jazz Festival was staged in 1980 and has continued with local, national and international bands and guests.

Opposite the Theatre Royal was the Pour House, a jazz venue that subsequently was Yesterdays, and now the Steam Rock Disco. During 1973 and early 1974 Roger Wells played there on drums with a band led by Henry Davies on piano. The other members of the band included Bob Mickleburgh,trumpet; Nick Cooper or Frank Fennell, clarinet; Pete Kendal, trombone; Gus Gander, or George Smith, sousaphone. The Severn Jazzmen also played there. This venue became Yesterdays and the Avon Cities were resident there in the early 1980s until it was damaged by fire.

The Naval Volunteer has also hosted jazz gigs, the Excelsior band having a regular spot there until another pub 'refurbishment' brought that to a close.

At the City Centre end of King Street was a low building, the Green Room. For a while it became the Avon Cities Club, until demolished in the early 1980s as part of a road widening scheme (see page 11). Roger Wells recalls playing there for a short time in 1974 with Bill Brown's Jazzmen, with Bill Brown on trumpet; Andy Leggett, clarinet; Bernie Newland, trombone; Q Williams, piano, and Roger on drums.

Information from Roger Wells
Editors

MUSICIANS TALES

LETTER FROM AMERICA

RAY BUSH

I purchased a clarinet in early 1947 when I was inducted into the army to do my National Service. Most of my time was spent in Feltham near London and as my father, due to illness, was an invalid, I was allowed a 48-hour pass every weekend. However, I could only afford to go home every two weeks so every other weekend I spent listening to Humph. When I came home I would be playing with Johnny Macey (guitar) above his father's sweetshop in Redcliffe Street, along with Conrad Gillespie (trombone) and Jay Hawkins. A couple of years later Johnny and Jay were members of Acker's band when he went professional in London. We spent many hours playing and listening to Bechet, Mezz and Tommy Ladnier above the sweetshop, with more that the occasional complaint from John's father to keep the noise down.

I was lucky to have a girlfriend in Feltham who took me to a pub in Cranford where I played with Ken Colyer. I could possibly be the first clarinet player to play with the Crane River Jazz Band (see the comments written by Monty Sunshine in the 100 club magazine around 1981).

After Demob I met the dance band leader Len Britton. He had what he called the Bristol Jazz Club in the Redcliffe Church Hall. That's where I first met Geoff Nichols (trumpet) and Brian Rushton who played the drums. He became our first band manager. During my army days I also played with a trumpet player from Bath called Joe Brickell. In his group were the pianist Glyn Wilcox and drummer Basil Wright. They became the original members of the Avon

A 1961 photograph of the Avon Cities band taken in the courtyard of Mike Hitchings house L to R: Ray Bush, Basil Wright, Geoff Nichols, Chris Marlowe (Sammi Brown), Frank Feeney, John Critchinson, Mike Hitchings and John Phipps.

Cities and it was Basil who thought up the band's name as the Avon flowed through both cities.

Geoff recalled, at the 50th anniversary concert, that the decision to form a band was taken above Johnny Macey's father's sweetshop and that sounds about right. One other thing I would like to mention, as I was manager of the band for about twenty years, is the behind the scene problems of managing a band. The man who managed the band from the early fifties through the sixties was Mike Bevan and a lot of credit is due to Mike for steering us through that very hectic period.

Edited excerpt from the 100 Club Magazine in the 1980s:

Monty Sunshine, alerted by Cy Laurie took his clarinet to Cranford where the Crane River Band, lead by Ken Colyer, held weekly sessions. Monty quotes, "Much to my dismay I found a clarinet player already blowing with the Cranes. I had just got out of the Royal Air Force and I remember he was still in uniform and playing pretty good! But luckily for me he was only stationed in the area for a short time and he was soon demobbed and went back home to Bristol. His name way Ray Bush, and it wasn't long before he was leading his own band, the Avon Cities Jazz Band."

Ray Bush

A ROUGH GUIDE.

MIKE COCKS

I was born in Bristol on the 4th July 1934 and thankfully still going. Parents both musical but gave their darling offspring no encouragement in that direction, nor did an expensive public school education help at all.

I started playing in 1956, with an old battered silver cornet which I bought for £2. I was robbed. I practised with a friend in the hollows on top of Dundry, where the bird population never forgave us.

In June 1956 I was the founder member of the Blue Note Jazzmen. Around this time I had lessons from Geoff Nichols for three months. I also borrowed £25 to buy a Holton trumpet/cornet, which I sold to [Flurge Appleyard] years later.

Our first public appearance was in December 1956. It must have sounded excruciatingly awful, but by God we had a nerve. None of us had been playing for more than nine months.

In 1958 I took Tony Osborne's trumpet chair in a band at Redland College. I was not a student there, but my future wife was. We met as a direct result of these sessions.

I briefly joined the Atlanta band in order to do a TV Gig on Brian Michie's "Now's your Chance" for TWW at their Pontcanna Studios, Cardiff. This was in 1959. I remember having a camera stuck up the bell of my horn, and having to tap in whilst holding the trumpet absolutely steady. A flood-light on top of the camera was making me exceptionally hot, and sweat was running down my face onto my mouthpiece. I was terrified that the horn was going to slip at the crucial moment, but it didn't, thank heavens. We entertained the passengers on the train on the way back to Bristol. They enjoyed it, but TWW were not impressed.

In August 1956 I joined Glyn Wilcox's Apex Jazz Band, based in Bath, and in 1960 some of us played for Jock Henderson's Dixieland All Stars from Cheltenham. The latter were also to play at the Bathurst, but Jock's inability to get to Bristol on time led to the formation of Mike Cocks' Chicagoans, with Dave Hibberd on drums in place of Jock.

Late in 1961 saw me depping for John Stainer in the Stainer/Collett 7 while he attended night school. This was a great band to play with and I always look back on those sessions with the fondest of memories.

In October 1962 I joined the Pearce Cadwallader Stompers, also based in Bath. This was a well-organised group with a manager (Tony Tavener) and rather smart uniforms, comprising light grey slacks, green single-breasted blazers and yellow ties. We had a lot of success around the Bath area under the cheerful leadership of Caddy. I stayed with the band until November 1963.

During this time I also played for the newly reformed Jeff Woodhouse band, taking Norman Hill's place. This gave me the chance to play Chicago style jazz as opposed to the New Orleans style of the Cadwallader band. During this period Jeff emigrated to Canada and dumped the band on my lap, where it became 'version two' of the Mike Cocks' Chicagoans for a short-lived spell. Oddly enough I can't recall a thing about this group except that we ended up with Richie Bryant on drums (who was later to join Acker Bilk) and Diane Mitchell sang with us, which was strange because I was normally averse to lady singers.

Mike Cocks, left, appearing with guest Danny Moss at the Duke.

In July 1965 I played with Henry's Bootblacks on third trumpet for a four month spell. This was my one and only attempt at big-band format, and as I was not a reader I found the third trumpet parts impossible to pick up by ear. However I did get to play the jazz solos and this was exciting, with a big sound to back one up.

In 1966 I became the founder member of the New Chicagoans. This was the band I stayed with until I retired in 1992. To me it was the most important band I ever played in. During most of this time there were countless gigs, guesting with other local bands, usually depping for the ubiquitous Flurge in either the Severn Jazzmen or Excelsior Jazzmen. On top of that there were other groups formed, usually based in the Old Duke, that came and went fairly rapidly. These were often designed to fill a vacant slot for Kon Aniol or John Stone, but not always. My favourite part time group rarely saw the light of day unfortunately, it was a quintet, usually composed of myself on trumpet, Don Burnell, tenor sax; Jack Toogood, guitar; Dave Hibberd, drums and Clive Morton, bass. This fulfilled my need to occasionally get away from the Dixieland/Mainstream set-up and just play straightforward uncluttered jazz. If I remember correctly we called the group Par Five, because our initial job was somewhere with sporting connotations. Later it became the Five of Us.

Funny Story Time

My only 'professional' gig was in December 1964, when Mike Bevan was called upon by Monty Sunshine to find a dep' trumpeter for the night, as he had just fired a 'now famous' trumpeter for being drunk and disorderly on stage, and hadn't had time to replace him. I apparently was the only guy available.

The job was at Ashley Down College of Technology and the start time was 7.30pm. I duly arrived at 7.15pm to find the whole place in pitch-blackness, so set off to find the nearest pub where I could relax for half an hour. Returned at 8pm - the place was in the dark, so back to the pub for another pint or two. Back to college at nine to find the lighting engineer but no one else. "No guv," I'm told, "nothing happening until at least 10.00." Back to the pub for another couple of pints. Just after 10 the band finally arrive and I make myself known to Monty. His first question to me is..."Where's the nearest pub?" "Follow me," I say, very confidently, and off I march with five strange musicians in tow. We only have time for two or three quick pints, drinking hours being what they were, which was as well because I realised I was getting horribly drunk. I tried to explain the story to Monty, just in case he thought all trumpet players got drunk before they played with his band, but he didn't seem worried.

We started playing at about 11pm. "You pick the numbers," said Monty to me, but my mind went blank. Fortunately, Graham Stewart (trombone) appreciated my alcoholic predicament and came to my rescue. We picked a number. "OK, tap it in," said Monty. "Who me?" "Yes." "But you're the bandleader." "Do it, for God's Sake," says Graham to me, "or we'll never get started!"

And so it went on. At the end of the evening Monty thanked me profusely for my help and duly paid me. But I wonder if I had been a regular member of his band whether he would have sacked me instead!

Mike Cocks

MAURICE REMEMBERS

MAURICE EVERSON

I remember jazz being played upstairs at the White Horse in Lower Ashley Road, St Pauls. I do not recall this being a jazz club, more of a meeting place for dance band players to get together to play jazz. If my memory serves me right some of the musicians were as follows: Bill Turner, tenor sax; Sid Uppington, bass; Duncan Wood, trumpet; Pete Olds, drums and Les Drake, piano.

In the 1950s and 1960s there was a club above a pub in Lawrence Hill. I believe one of the organisers was a guy named Freddy Floyd. The music style was mainstream to modern and meetings were on Thursday evenings with many musicians turning up to 'sit in'.

Jazz enthusiasts will remember the Dugout club in Park Row in the 1960s, with musicians turning up after their respective dance gigs on Saturday nights. I recall playing with the Frank Evans Band at various venues with Bill Taylor on piano, Alan Close, and Ian Hobbs on drums.

London musicians were frequent and welcome visitors to Bristol. Names that spring to mind are Ronnie Ross, Joe Harriot, Shake Keone, and at the British Restaurant on College Green, none other than the great Tubby Hayes.

Maurice Everson

Maurice, aged 20 years, performing at the Roost Club, Lawrence Hill, 1950.

STORMIN' NORMAN

NORMAN HILL

Norman has had a close affinity with the U.S.A. having been there many times. The first time was illegally, having crossed the border from Canada. When asked why? Norman replied that all the bars were closed in Toronto on Sundays! This was in 1948, Norman having emigrated to Canada looking for work.

Like many other Jazz musicians Norman started learning to play the piano as a boy. He was also listening keenly and being influenced by Jazz musicians such as Louis Armstrong and 'home grown' Nat Gonella. At 15 his mother gave him a trumpet and he started lessons with a local teacher, Glyn Davis.

In 1942 Norman went to work in Gloucester and his trumpet teacher there conducted the Rotol Brass Band. He invited Norman to join the band, playing cornet. Norman recalls Sir George Dowty encouraging the band by buying them tea at rehearsals. Norman also played in a Dance Band during his time in Gloucester.

At the end of World War II Norman returned to Bristol and played in the brass section of the ACES Dance Band (Association for Community, Education and Sport). This band had three trumpets, three trombones, six saxophones, and a vocalist and rhythm section. They played at the Wills Recreation Hall and church halls and they also formed smaller bands for Dances. Geoff Parton was the first trumpet and a very good player. However, Norman took the solos.

Things seemed to be going very well musically when disaster struck. On one occasion while playing at the Wills Hall, Bedminster, Norman's lip packed up, even before the interval. He could not get to playing again for two weeks. Something had to be done. He found a good teacher in London, Mr Phil Parker Snr. Norman had weekly lessons with him in Soho and learned breathing techniques as well as developing his embouchure. This represented a large investment as the weekly cost of £1 per session and the return fare to London was 7/6. At this time Norman played occasional Jazz gigs at Bristol University, with Jan Ridd on piano, Graham Rogers on drums and Pete Brothers on clarinet.

Norman emigrating to Canada in January 1948 interrupted these very important lessons with Phil Parker. Norman played while he was there and also found a music teacher but he did not stay there long as, through a friend he found a job back in London. There he resumed his lessons and started playing with Derek Wood's band, which was short of a trumpet player. Derek Woods played soprano sax and clarinet. This band was quickly to become the Norman Hill Jazz Band, and they played at the Cooks Ferry Inn, The 100 Club in Oxford Street and the Albert Hall among other venues. Norman also at this time played with Beryl Bryden's Backroom Boys, Graeme Bell's band and Mick Mulligan's band, on tour. He once played with Humphrey Lyttelton at a concert at the Croydon Civil Hall, and 'Humph' returned the compliment by playing with Norman's band. Although Norman played with many of the big names in jazz he never turned professional as by then he had a steady job and a family to support.

In August 1962 Norman returned to Bristol to live and soon became reintegrated into the Bristol jazz scene. He joined the Blue Note Jazz Band for a while and played with the Severn Jazzmen, as well as in his own quartet at the Old Duke on Thursday nights. The quartet had Jan Ridd on piano, Bob Riddiford on bass and Dave Jackson on drums. Norman also played with Henry's Bootblacks and while Geoff Nichols was absent from the Avon Cities band, studying for a degree, Norman took over the trumpet lead.

As a diversion, Norman in the 1970s played regularly at the

Norman Hill and Charlie Shavers performing at the Granary in November 1969. A night to remember.

Globetrotters Club, Clifton, with the Ewart Niblett Trio; vibes, bass and drums. They played the long intervals between the striptease acts. Norman particularly remembers a beautiful 'Zulu' stripper (wouldn't he just) and of course he met Big Julie, later to be immortalised in song by Dave Collett.

During the heyday of Jazz at the Granary in November '69, Norman played there with Charlie Shavers. As Norman had previously met Charlie in Toronto he was deputed to meet him from the train at Temple Meads Station and to take him to the Royal Hotel. Charlie had long been one of Norman's heroes as one of the world's foremost trumpet players and so he was delighted to have the opportunity to swap experiences of people and places they both had known in Canada and the USA, and a firm friendship was struck. That evening performance at the Granary was to become one of the really great musical experiences of his life as Charlie invited Norman to play a duet with him. The number chosen was "Undecided" one of Charlie's own, and the exiting performance brought the house down. Much later, on a visit to the U.S.A. Charlie pre-

sented Norman with his trumpet mouthpiece, a treasured memento to this day.

Perhaps Bristol Jazz followers will best remember Norman Hill for his long residency with Rod Coleman's Six-Piece Suite, a regular Sunday night slot at the Old Duke for many years. This piano-led band of talented musicians was an urbane and happy combination. Rod's piano playing, stylish vocals and disarming smile set the relaxed humorous musical style, and Norman provided the uninhibited bravura. His 100% plus performances never failed to hit the high notes, and for the Sunday-nighters it kept those 'Monday morning blues' at bay.

Editor's interviews with Norman Hill

MIND YOUR ARSE ON THE STEP!

JOHN HOPKINS

Circa 1978, the New Chicagoans enjoyed a regular Wednesday at the Malt and Hops in Broad Street. It was a well attended and popular venue, with some great supporters. The banter that went on between the band and the punters was at it's usual best. Two of our regulars were Roger and his wife, 'Paddy', who were always ready for a laugh. (Unfortunately, Paddy is no longer with us, but is always remembered).

One night during a particularly lengthy run of banter, I rejoined "MIND YER ARSE ON THE STEP!" Paddy fell about laughing, and at the end of the session she asked me about it. I told her that it wasn't my expression, but that of a Liverpudlian named Jess Whitehurst with whom I had some dealings at work. The following Wednesday at the end of the session, I closed with the same words, which had the same result.

One week later, at the close, Paddy was looking directly at me, waiting for me to say it, which I did. Not only had it now stuck fast, but the whole band picked it up, and it became our closing chorus, as it still is today.

So, it's "Goodnight, from the New Chicagoans, God Bless, and don't forget"................'the rest is history.'

John Hopkins

A LIFE OF BRIAN

BRIAN HUGGETT

Brian has had the happy propensity during his Jazz career of being much in demand. He has played with many Jazz and Dance bands during his long career which started with the West of England College of Art band in 1954.

During service in the RAF (1956-1957) he was a member of the RAF Military Band and then on return to Bristol he had a short spell with Gerry Bath's Apex Jazz Band and the Jubilaires. He was also with the Alan Davis Jazzmen until 1960.

Between 1959 and 1964 Brian played in the following bands: the Roy Reed Jazzmen; The Imperial Jazzband and the Pearce Cadwallader Stompers, a very busy person. From 1964 Brian joined the reed section of Henry's Bootblacks, playing Henry's classical style Jazz of the 1920s and 1930s. He was on the Bootblacks first recording in 1965.

1968 saw the start of an association that has lasted over thirty years when Brian joined Dave Millman's Severn Jazzmen. He has featured in all their recordings.

The early 1970s found Brian with Bobby Mickelburgh's All British Dance Orchestra, and in the mid 1970s with stints in the Panama Jazz Band, King Street 7 and the Magnificent 7. From 1974-76 Brian was with Mike Cocks' New Chicagoans and the start of another long-term association began in 1977 with Brian joining Mike Cooper's Excelsior Jazz Band. Around this time further bands requested his presence and performance; Q Williams' band, the Louisiana Jazz Kings, the Apex Jazz Band and the Riverside Jazzmen.

On the 20th December 1980 the trumpeter Bob Wade formed a band to play under his name at the Old Duke on alternate Saturday nights. In April 1981 the band was renamed the Six Piece Suite and played in the Old Duke on Sunday nights until January 1995. Brian played throughout the whole duration of the band.

From 1980 onwards Brian could be seen legging it around Bristol and surrounding areas, usually in the big outdoors with the Great Western Marching Band. He was also for a time, in the late 1980s, with Alice's Wonderland Band, and in October 1988 formed and led the Delta Four. They had a residency at the Shakespeare in Redland playing the first Tuesday of each month over a period of four years. During that time they had on trumpet Norman Hill and Tony Osborne, John Viner on guitar and banjo and Bob Riddiford on bass. Sometimes instead of bass, Jeremy (Brian's son) would play electric piano, or in place of trumpet Jeremy would play tenor sax or flute.

Brian's influences on clarinet were Benny Goodman and Artie Shaw. On alto sax, he was influenced initially by Benny Carter and Johnny Hodges, followed later by Paul Desmond. Brian has appeared with many leading UK jazz musicians including Nat Gonella, Harry Gold, George Chisholm, Danny Moss and Roy Williams. He has played live on both television and radio and has toured and performed at many UK and continental jazz clubs and festivals. These have included the prestigious Guinness Festival at Cork, Den Bosch and Breda in Holland and Ghent in Belguim. Two separate memorable occasions were when he played alongside the legendary American tenor sax player Bud Freeman, and later the American stride pianist Ralph Sutton. Brian was for two consecutive years voted the winner on clarinet, soprano and alto sax in a jazz poll conducted

May 1968. Brian on alto sax. Photograph taken at a once popular jazz venue, the New Passage Hotel, Pilning. Brian was performing with the New Chicagoans.

by the Bath Chronicle newspaper.

Brian's busy and extensive jazz career reflects in some ways the Bristol jazz scene over the years, with many musicians moving around the bands which form and reform. Some had brief lives, others lasting for several years, and some still happily carrying on.

Compiled from information supplied by Brian Huggett
Editor

101

A PIANIST'S TALE

ALAN HURLEY

Alan learned to play the piano from the age of seven and by seventeen was beginning to play jazz. His first efforts in public began with a dance band, playing with a drummer and accordion player to packed dances in village halls all over the West Country. None of these premises were licensed - people brought their own beer and sandwiches and the band used to go to the nearest pub for refreshments during the interval.

Later the Roost Jazz Club was started in Old Market and Alan played there with various line-ups, playing what was known at the time as 'Swing Music' or modern jazz. A regular trio was Alan on piano, Sid Uppington on bass and Kloop Cox on drums. Guests playing with the trio included Phil Seaman from the Jack Parnell band, Tubby Hayes on tenor, Eric Delaney on drums and Jimmy Skidmore (tenor), whose son Alan Skidmore is still famously playing tenor sax. Jimmy claimed to be able to belch "God Save the Queen".

At around this time Eddie Thompson, a piano player who was blind used to stay with Alan, who recalls the time when Eddie was playing in a cabaret club for a stripper. When the strip started Eddie's guide dog went up on stage, sat next to the stripper and howled throughout the act.

Big Bands were very popular then and Alan played for the Raymond Kay Band based in Weston. This band had around 17 - 20 members and played regularly at venues all around the Bristol area. A weekly slot for years was at Bristol South Baths, which was attended by audiences of several hundred people. There were sometimes fights and a heavy police presence was at hand around the corner to charge in when a whistle was sounded. Troublemakers were pushed unceremoniously through the heavy doors and were often stunned by the time they reached the 'Black Maria'. Tear gas was used on one occasion but the band was urged to keep playing whatever happened.

The Raymond Kay Band was a very professional outfit with the same agent as the Eric Winstone Big Band. Within the band were a trad group and a modern group so that the band could alternate styles to suit the 'Jivers' or 'Boppers' in the audience, and they contrived to play continuously throughout the evening. The band also played at the Pier and the Winter Gardens in Weston and at American Army camps, where the majority of the patrons were so swamped with entertainment that they scarcely listened to anything.

There was plenty of work for musicians in the early 50's and as well as the Big Band Alan played in a trio at the Frying Pan restaurant where his wife June was offered a job as a waitress, as the only way she could see him in the evenings!
Alan spent 8 years with the Raymond Kay Band and during this time the band won the South West and Wales sections of the Melody Maker competitions three years running, and went up to Belle View Circus in Manchester for the finals. Ted Heath's band was the house band on one occasion and Alan enjoyed the contact with many first class musicians. On one occasion Alan won the piano score award.

After the big band, from about 1959 Alan played with Jack Toogood's Quartet. This band played at the Grand Hotel, the Spa, and Pontins Holiday camp as well as other venues. The line up included Alan Aplin on bass and Peter Wemyss on drums, with Alan on piano and Jack on guitar. The quartet recorded and performed for the BBC, being heard on programmes such as 'Spotlight' and 'Tap Your Feet'. Bunny

Alan Hurley, piano, playing with the Jack Toogood Quartet. Photograph taken at Sand Bay 1959. L to R: Jack Toogood, Peter Wemyss, Alan Avlin and Alan.

Millar sang with them - he also sang with the Raymond Kay Big Band, and still sings with the Tony Stone Band at the Little Thatch, and with the Dave Salt Band (which is a rehearsal band now).

Alan recalls being paid quarterly by Jack Toogood and that the money was very good by today's standards. Musicians could pick up work at recruiting venues such as Brown's Music Shop where bandleaders congregated to attract the best players they could get.

Jazz was played at the Co-op Hall in Terrell Street, St. Mary Redcliffe, and at various pubs in that area. Traditional and modern jazz was separated at the insistence of the patrons - musicians were often keen to play in different styles. Alan also played with the Jack Aston Quintet with Maurice Everson, bass; Alan Close, trumpet; Ian Hobbs, drums, and Jack on tenor sax. This group made recordings in 1956.

Alan joined the New Chicagoans in the mid-eighties after the very sad demise of the much-loved Les Drake. Alan played with this band at the Old Duke until his death in January 2000.

Other bands, which Alan had joined, included the Jazz Factory, which started in the early eighties and played at pubs such as the Bull at Hinton, the Plume at Hotwells and the Albert Inn, Bedminster. He had also played at the Dugout Club where musicians used to go after sessions at the Spa Hotel to jam into the small hours.

Not many Bristol musicians were part of the drugs scene, although of course those like Alan who travelled with their band often saw at close hand the havoc that this wreaked else-where.

Piano players until quite recently had to make do with the instruments provided by the venue, whereas their colleagues took with them their cared for and cherished instruments.

Even today a number of pianists are not that happy with the portable electric piano but use it as an alternative as a lot of pianos are just too awful to contemplate playing.

Alan, in common with other pianists had a collection of horror stories about arriving at gigs to find a piano, as Oscar Peterson once related "You wouldn't give to your grandmother for fire wood"! A couple of Alan's stories about piano inci-

Another 1959 photograph with Alan at the piano; note the early electric keyboard under his right hand.

dents are worth repeating here.

Some years ago Alan was booked to play at a well known Bristol girls school, where the assembly hall had been booked. The stage piano was so out of tune that it could not be played with the other band instruments. The organisers of the event contacted the headmistress who forbade the use of the grand piano to play jazz. However the students who had organised the do were not deterred, Alan had come, and he should play. They decided to lift the grand from the floor of the hall on to the stage. Alan said it was entirely up to them. Alan never got to play that piano as in getting it on to the stage it was not lifted high enough and the legs and pedals were unceremoniously snapped off. The conclusion of this incident is unknown, perhaps too painful to relate.

There was once a gig at a military establishment near Bath where Alan's band had been booked to play. He had a contract that stated that there would be a piano and in tune. On arrival there was no piano and the entertainment's officer, (usually the most junior Lt.) said there was no problem as there seemed to be other musicians with instruments. Alan pointed out that it was his band and he had a contract to say there would be piano and in any case he wished to play. Eventually the Commanding Officer was called and was not too happy about all this but eventually said Alan could use the grand piano that he had in his home.

Alan was pleased at this suggestion not realising that the piano was being pushed by a posse of squaddies on it's own wheels for at least half a mile and then across the drill square. On opening the keyboard and playing a couple of chords the effect was like dropping a crate of empty beer bottles into a harp. Alan said "I can't play this" to which the C O, perhaps not realising that his grand might be ruined for ever replied, "There's no pleasing you chappies"!

At Alan's funeral at Bath in January 2000 there was a very large gathering of jazz musicians and followers, a reflection of the high esteem and affection in which Alan was held.

Editors interview with Alan Hurley

.

GOIN' OUT THE BACK WAY

TONY OSBORNE

SETTING OUT.......

Do you remember the Y.W.C.A. Gym at the top of Great George Street? It was there in the early fifties that many of us got our first taste of real, live Jazz. Here before our very eyes and ears was a manifestation of those sounds which we had hitherto only heard through a mist of hiss and pop as we crouched over our 'Dansettes' or portable wind-ups, frowning to catch every note and nuance of performances by Jelly Roll, King Oliver,or Blind Lemon Jefferson.

I cannot recall from whom I first heard about the 'Summer House', the Avon Cities Jazz Club. I had been listening to jazz records for some time before I finally made the pilgrimage to the top of Great George Street. I tentatively entered, clutching my half-crown, and discovered a kind of noisy paradise. I was of course very young, and very unsure of myself. The Band, doing the very thing I wished to do more than anything else in the world, consisted of folk I had heard spoken of in hushed tones, folk I may say who seemed then to be so much older than I, and so much more sophisticated, and dare I say it, unapproachable. Most of them are now among those I am grateful to call friends and contemporaries. Why is a relatively small age difference so significant when one is young, and so unimportant when one is old?

Jazz, as far as I was concerned, was of course for listening. However, the Club had already discovered that there were those who preferred dancing, and who were prepared to pay to do it to the right kind of music. So there were dancers. After all, Jazz was essentially dance music, although those of us who saw Rudy Blesh as our Guru were not altogether convinced. We looked upon the music as an art-form, dancing was sacrilege, a kind of denial of the improvisatory creative instinct. It certainly did not dawn on me to question the 'Master', even though I did know somewhere in the back of my mind that the original players, even the likes of Johnny Dodds and Louis Armstrong, were basically earning their living by playing this music. Musicians soon learn that if you are doing it to live, you play what people want to hear. We swept such pragmatic concepts from your minds. Jazz was almost a religion.

On this first visit, I stood in awe of the place, the band, the other people, the lady on the door, indeed of every vibrating atom of the experience. It was my first attempt at socialisation, and it was marvellous. In time, I learned to watch and listen and learn, for I was determined one day to be up there playing jazz too. I found myself ignoring and detesting with some vehemence the swirling figures in front of the stage, silhouetted against the backdrop of New Orleans wrought-iron balconies, painted I discovered later, by Mike Hitchings. It did not even enter my mind that they were worshipping at their altar too.

The 'Summer House' was dark, a bit smelly, and quite without convenience of any kind. It did not matter one whit. It was exciting, noisy, warm, and THE place to worship in. We worshipped the traditional line-up; we worshipped the famous names; we worshipped the tunes we recognised from the 'Brunswick' and 'Parlophone' labels we played at home; we revered Geoff Nichols, Ray Bush, The Prof, Bas Wright, Mike Hitchins and Jan Ridd. Later we added Wayne Chandler when he joined the band, and the band joined the 'Skiffle' movement. We firmly believed that 'Skiffle' was a true derivative of the blues. Perhaps we were not as discriminating as we thought.

Tony, performing with the New Chicagoans, at a gig in Broad Street, 1979.

Attendance at the 'Summer House' was an education both in music and in life. Here we listened obsessively, to the music, that by discovery, we had brought back from the dead. But it did not end there. It was here we formulated our first ideas about Life, Art and Politics. Here I first heard the names Henry James, T.S.Eliot and Aldous Huxley. The interval was an evening class of culture, even if it was all above my head.

This unexpected phenomenon was due largely to one man. A man around whom we tyros clustered as if around a prophet. A man who proclaimed wisdom's between puffs of 'Players'

smoke, which fired our imaginations beyond reason, and all without a drink or the ingestion of strange substances. The 'Summer House' worked its magic on us all through the medium of jazz, and the wisdom of one T.K.Daniel.

THE FOUNDRY INN

There comes a time when an all-consuming interest demands of its captive the need to actively participate in its production. Train-spotters become 'Railway Enthusiasts'; Aeroplane nuts become pilots, and listeners to Jazz Records become frantic to have a go at being a Jazz Musician. So it was with me. I could not believe my luck when a school friend who, for medical reasons, no longer wished to go on playing the trumpet, offered it to me to learn on. I leapt at the chance. With little or no idea about how to become a Jazz Trumpeter, I set about learning to blow.

I have never been a one to do things properly. Not for me the traditional path of seeking lessons from a trumpet teacher. I had read Rudy Blesh, several times, and taking lessons from folk was not how I believed Jazz Players did it. The thing was to teach yourself. That I fervently believed was how the pioneers did it. But how? It should not prove difficult I thought, music was about in our house. We had a piano, my mother was a music teacher, I myself had reached 'The Gavotte from Mignon' before setting my face against classical style piano and resigning from the trials of keyboard practice.

It seemed a logical thing. One played a note on the piano, and blew around on the trumpet until one found the corresponding tone. Do that for all the notes and.... well it must be a cinch! For me it appeared so. For my parents and the neighbours it must have been akin to hell. But I persisted, and they were very kind. It was many years later I made the discovery that this was not the best approach, but by that time I had acquired all the worst instrumental habits possible.

The trumpet was very old, and the mouthpiece was very small and flat. I knew nothing about the role of the mouthpiece then, so as I blew the tones came out very loud and very high. I learned to play "When the Saints Go Marching In" so high that the top notes were almost beyond audible range for humans. (The neighbours must have prayed for those passages when all went quiet for a second or two).

Having at least achieved a repertoire, (of one tune), the next step was to form a band. Now this was beyond my organisational abilities at the time, so it was with great pleasure that, through the grapevine, someone who needed a trumpeter heard that I was in possession of a trumpet. The word came to contact the Vieux Carre Jazz Band for an audition at the Foundry Inn, in Newfoundland Road. I did the necessary contacting. The band was run by one Roger Bennett, a former Junior School mate who was known to me, although he had been a year older and therefore unapproachable at the time. The fact that his dad had been 'Uncle Bob' of the Evening Post Pillar Box Club, of which I had been a member in my younger days, added a certain piquancy to the situation.

Now, I had never been in a Pub. Lads of sixteen did not go into Pubs in those days, because of the age limits. In any case, Pubs then were not the social meeting places they are today. Pubs, especially in Newfoundland Road, were dark sinister dens, smelling excitingly of tobacco and stale George's Ales, full of old men who did not take kindly to strangers. There was no doubt at all that my father would not have been too pleased had he known that I was heading for a rendezvous in a Pub. By a stroke of luck one of the members of the Vieux Carre Band was the son of a wealthy local businessman who owned a factory or two, and he drove a car. To get to be a passenger in a car in those days was exceptional to say the least. This in the event was what happened. The car with the lads in it arrived, and after brief introductions we drove off to the Foundry Inn.

The Pub was old and dark and as exciting inside as I had imagined it would be. In olden days pubs had a certain smell which is not evident today, a smell of good ale, old smoke and age. A dark, inviting smell redolent of something vaguely to do with the seamy side of life. We went in and mounted the stairs to the upper room. It was also dark and big and high ceilinged. On one wall was a huge buffalo head, symbol of the 'Royal Ancient Order of Buffaloes', who met, I later found out, in the room for official meetings.

We got down to business. "What can you play?" asked Roger. "The Saints", I replied. "That will do for a start", he replied. Geoff Pugh the piano player began, and I started to play. It was terrible. There was a lot of wincing and tolerant grimacing. I finished, and there was silence. "You play very loud", said one, "and very high", said another. "Lets try something else", said someone else, and thus the evening progressed.

We sent down for some beer after a bit. This was a first too. It was an exciting evening. It got even more exciting when it was decided that despite my almost total ineptitude, I was asked to play with the band. Heaven had come to Bristol! I was a member of a Jazz Band! We drove home, I think, I was too far off the ground to tell. Little did I then think that I was on the road which was to effect the entire rest of my life, not always for the best. The die was cast. The first of my ambitions was achieved. I was to be a Jazzman.

CORVINUS RECORDS

T.K.Daniel was something of a man of authority to youngsters like myself, just setting out on their journey into the Bristol Jazz World, and anxious to arrive. I simply wanted to know all there was to know about the music and its history, ensnared as I was by the magic of it, and T.K. or 'Tikky' as he came to be known, appeared to be the possessor of an endless fund of esoteric information about jazz and thus the fountainhead I sought. I did not know where he came from, how he had acquired this apparent knowledge, or even approximately how old he was. To me and my friends, just learning the trade, Tikky was the man to be seen with. The Guru within whose sphere it was our ambition to be.

Tikky was not stinting with his knowledge. Every jazz night at the Summer House he could be heard expounding loudly above the music, some obscure point of discographical truth, his beard, fingers and teeth brown with the passage of many, many cigarettes, his hands and arms gesticulating widely and his voice distinctively angular and percussive. He gave the impression of an academic of the old school, surrounded by his acolytes, dispensing wisdom as if there was no question whatsoever concerning the truth of his utterances.

There was no doubt about it, if one was to be in the swim, access to the circle of Tikky's acquaintances was a goal to be achieved. To such as myself, all young and as eager as any newly awakened jazz enthusiast to attain a similar pinnacle of authority, some way had to be found to break into the circle. The hero practitioners of our enthusiasm were at a distance from us, or so it seemed. One approached them with some trepidation as an outsider to an insider. The gap was of our making, not theirs, but then, we were younger than they were, and in those days, age assumed an importance which it no longer has. On jazz club evenings, it was rather as if the Court of Louis XVI was passing by, one hoped to be recognised by the King, and if one was, it was a step in the right direction. Thus we clustered around Tikky like apostles around a Messiah, hoping to be noticed.

It was known that Tikky ran what was euphemistically called a 'Record Shop' at number 71 Horfield Road. It was my tremendous luck on one famous occasion to be invited to go to the shop with one Alan Crang, the school friend who had introduced me to jazz in the first place. Alan was a bit older than I was, and thus had something of a head start in the 'getting to know Tikky' stakes. For me this was exciting stuff. Could this invitation be seen as a step along the road to achieving my goal?.....I eagerly accepted.

We arrived at number 71. It was dark and a bit grubby on the outside. The windows were impenetrable because they were covered all over with record sleeves from old 78's, the ones with large holes in the middle. The shop was called 'Corvinus Records'. The reference to 'crows' was not apparent until one passed through the door and came into the barren, black interior of the shop, which resembled more a bare room than any kind of business premise.

We went in. The shop was almost bare. There was a counter of sorts, but it seemed that the purpose of the place was to accommodate a number of people who were just sitting around talking. Of a record stock there seemed to be none. There were many boxes and old record covers to match the windows, but it was not a 'record shop' as I understood the term. We sat down after perfunctory greetings, which briefly interrupted Tikky in mid-flow as he made a pronouncement concerning the recording of something by somebody, and the peculiar circumstances of the event. His speech cut through the cloud of cigarette smoke which filled the place, almost obscuring the faces of the other members of the audience. I recognised some as local jazz musicians and enthusiasts, and was gratified to be nodded at by one or two. I thought at that moment that I had arrived. I began to believe that I was at last part of the 'inner sanctum', a member of the jazz fraternity. It was epoch-making stuff!

One event from that day always stuck in my mind as illustrating the unique nature of Tikky and 'Corvinus Records'. Here was a record shop. Here was a record dealer. Here was a crowd of people sitting in what did not appear in the least to be what it purported to be, discussing the details of jazz and all its esoteric grandeur, under the watchful and critical eye of a knowledgeable man. Suddenly the shop door opened, and in came a stranger. At once the talking stopped, and all faces turned to examine the intruder who had interrupted the flow. He glanced at us, embarrassed by the sudden silence, and went towards what he took to be the counter. Tikky turned towards him with a questioning countenance.

"Do you have a record of Louis Armstrong playing "Sweethearts on Parade'?" asked the stranger.

"No". replied Tikky shortly, as if the young man had asked for something obscene.

There was a pause of some moments. "But I can probably get you a copy of Bob Crosby".

"Oh" said the young man. "I really wanted it by Louis Armstrong".

There was another pause, during which no sound was made, and the stranger turned and fled before the combined gaze of the 'in-crowd'.

Tikky turned back to face us, "Did you hear about the trumpet player on one of the early Ellington sessions who caught his fingers in the studio door and had to be replaced by a visiting viola player from San Francisco, who happened to be passing by? "Well............"

It was as if nothing had disturbed the peace and tranquillity of our little world. It was no good coming in thinking you could buy a record, of all things. You had to earn your entrée to 'Corvinus Records'.

GOIN' OUT THE BACK WAY

Do you remember 'Stan's Record Shop'? It lurked above Blake's Medical Stores in Denmark Street, and for a number of years was a meeting place for many of Bristol's Jazzers. Occasionally somebody bought a record, but more often than not, folk just hung around and talked about Jazz. 'Stan's' holds a special place in my heart, for it was there that I spent my college days when I should have been writing learned essays, not listening to the latest disc, taking advice from the man himself, or chatting to Vi, Mrs Strickland. 'Stan's' opened at a crucial period in my life, a carefree student in the mid-flush of intending to become a teacher, playing most evenings in the band, and effecting to be a aficionado of the art of Jazz music.

'Stan's' as I have said, was situated above Blake's Medical Stores, so going in and coming out required a swerving technique which would leave an observer in no doubt as to which shop one was entering or leaving. Even at that time, I was never quite sure what Blake's sold, I was convinced it was not simply aspirin and cough medicine, but precisely what was so 'interesting' about Blake's I did not know, and did not like to ask.

I went past Stan's former shop the other day. It was a sad experience, for now it sits derelict and blind over an equally derelict and boarded-up late 'speedy' shoe repairers. No echo remains of the Mecca it once was. There was a time when you could still see the place where the shop sign hung - no more - it has all gone. 'Stan's' is now only a memory, a very fond memory, for it played its unique part in my life as a Jazz gigster. We had been playing what we rather pretentiously called 'Jazz' around the area for a few years, and had joined Gerry Bath's Climax Jazzband after the demise of the Vieux Carre following an unsuccessful take-over bid by one of Bristol's more capable musicians. The Climax was a different kettle of fish from previous efforts. It was lead by a piano player, who knew what he was doing rather better than we did, knew what he was aiming for and how to achieve it, and furthermore he was a dab hand at producing original works, which was quite a departure at that time.

The band consisted of Gerry Bath, leader and piano; Brian Williams, banjo; Tony Young, drums; the late Mark Burnham, trombone and sousaphone; Roger Bennet, clarinet and soprano, and myself, trumpet. The Climax' played many gigs around the place, we even made a record with Stan Strickland one evening in the shop. At the recording session, the larger part of the Band arranged itself around the empty sales room and out on the stairs, according to loudness , while Stan set up his microphones and tape-recorder in his small back room. We recorded a number of tunes, including fluffs, downright mistakes and swearing. We even included some of our leader's original numbers, "The Stance" and "Gerry's Blues" were two examples. The next day we watched, fascinated, as Stan transferred the tape onto an 'acetate' via his disk-cutting machine which whirled away, creating huge webs of swarf, covering the floor and shelves. It was like magic. I have a copy of that record. I am sure it will be a collector's piece one day.

Stan was a source of great encouragement to the likes of us who spent most of our waking hours in his shop. We had no money, so we didn't buy much, just hung around, but felt we were part of the scene. The net result of all this chatting and dawdling was that names got about and from time to time we were asked to 'Dep' for the great and good of the Bristol Jazz scene - Thank you Stan!

For me there was a small cloud on the horizon. I knew somewhere in the back of my mind that the end of college was approaching, and the question of passing the course was becoming a matter of frequent and heated comment at mealtimes at home. All this hanging around Stan's was fine, but it didn't help towards obtaining a useful qualification. The question of The Future was frequently referred to in quite marked tones by my father. National Service had come and gone, College was here, and now what? The possibility of spending the rest of my life playing the trumpet didn't even enter the frame. Teaching was seen to be a solid, secure, permanent, pensionable, reliable thing to be doing. "So lets hear no more of this Jazz nonsense", I almost heard my father thinking. But why teaching of all things? I was no great shakes at school, indeed I had left not so much under a cloud as inside one. They didn't even know I had gone and I am sure they didn't care. I had left school somewhat hastily, and had secured a post with a paint manufacturers as an office boy, (the junior one - the senior one was to become someone of note in the building trade in due course - we are still pals) but this was not what I foresaw as my life's work.

After very little inner debate, I had decided that my priorities were to get a job that paid reasonably well, which allowed a fair amount of time to be devoted to Jazz, and which had long holidays. Several of my Jazzy friends had got to grips with this dilemma and had chosen to go to college to become teachers - this was obviously the thing to do! There was at that time something of a shortage of teachers so I applied, was interviewed, and just before going off to defend the realm against the foreign foe, sealed my fate by agreeing to go to college and eventually emerge, fates being willing, (and they nearly weren't - but that's another story) a qualified teacher. I gave the whole affair no more thought than that.
And thus it turned out. I returned from the battlefield to college, where we started a Jazz band, entertained the students instead of writing essays, and illustrated learned addresses on

such topics as The Life and Times of Humphrey Lyttelton. The place was oozing with Jazz musicians. Jazz was THE music of the time. Life was good. I did no work, got engaged, nearly got thrown out, but I did play Jazz and hang around in Stan's, and life WAS good.

Then one day in 1958, after spending a lazy afternoon at Stan's, reality suddenly struck with all the force of a well flung half-brick. The college course came to an end in a month's time and this carefree life would be over. I was virtually a married man. I had to qualify and I had to get a job - well, that was what one did. I was 22.

It was head-down time, and after one of the most touch and go episodes of my life, I passed my final exams and became a qualified teacher - but only just. My fiancé and I got some serious discussion time in and we decided to go to London, where teaching jobs were plentiful. To my surprise I obtained an appointment. It was the end of play, it was time to leave the playground.

The day before we caught the train to Paddington, I went to say goodbye to Stan and Vi. It was a sad parting. I returned home, regretfully to put my 'Selmer Invicta' into it's box for the last time, and put it away in the cupboard..............it never came out again.

But then, twenty years later ....

Tony Osborne

STRINGALONG

JACK TOOGOOD

How young can you be to start depping for another musician? Jack depped in St. George for Les Drake on the Bethel Young Mens Bible Class American organ when he was thirteen years of age. Jack had learnt to play the piano, starting at the age of seven, although he confesses that he didn't have a real interest in keyboard instruments, adding that it's a great basis for learning other instruments.

George Formby became an important figure in Jack's early life, becoming smitten with the ukulele craze after seeing some of George Formby's films and listening to the recordings. Jack taught himself with the aid of all the tutors he could get hold of. He admits that during his teenage years he just lived for the ukulele. After leaving school at fifteen Jack started work as a junior clerk in an insurance office. As junior clerk his job entailed delivering local letters. Passing a newsagents he noticed a copy of B M G (Banjo Mandolin and Guitar) monthly magazine devoted to stringed instruments. Thinking that there might be something in it to learn more about his beloved ukulele Jack bought his first copy. He remembers the date as January 1940.

Two months later he was taking lessons on plectrum guitar from Horace Craddy who had advertised in the B M G magazine. Jack stayed with Horace until he was called up into the army in November 1942. The real basis of Jack's career came from Horace Craddy who made him aware of Lang, Kress, McDonough, and later Django Reinhardt. Jack started collecting the records of these famous guitarists, which have so influenced his own style.

Studying for insurance exams at the same time as learning the guitar was not easy and the former profession did not stand much of a chance.

When call-up came Jack took his guitar with him into the army and managed to practice and take part in impromptu sessions. With peace in Europe Jack's unit was in Germany and he was transferred to the Brigade Concert Party 103 A A Brigade Royal Artillery. When the unit was disbanded he was fortunate in being posted to the 49th Division Roadshow, the "Polar Stars" commanded by Lt.Hugh Paddick of radio comedy and "Carry On" film fame. Jack recalls that it was excellent training for him as there were many fine musicians in the band, Don Lusher being one of them.

By this time Jack had gone electric, his guitar being electrified by the good offices of the R E M E workshops. While playing with the "Polar Stars" Jack experienced his first broadcast. This was from the British Forces Network Hamburg, where with the "Polar Stars" he did a week of broadcasting, an experience that was to prove invaluable later back in the U K.

On demobilisation, and back in Bristol Jack decided not to return to the insurance company he had left on call-up. The same salary as before he left, and the thought of a life in insurance convinced him that he should become a professional musician. It was very hard for a time but Jack soon gained a reputation as a guitar teacher and in 1947 he started the Blue Star Quintet with Les Drake, who introduced him to Don Burnell, who was an accomplished reed player (tenor sax and clarinet). With Norman Cole on bass and Sid Barnes on drums the Blue Star Quintet had their first gig in the Bristol area. In 1950 the Quintet did a broadcast from the Bristol BBC studios playing numbers which included "Sweet Georgia Brown" and "What's This".

The Quintet became the Mac McCoombe Quintet when Mac joined. He was from London and played violin in the Joe Venuti style. The first recording as the Mac MaCoombe Quintet was from the studios of the BBC London. The programme was "Jazz Club" and broadcast on the 29th July 1950. Humphrey Lyttelton and his band were also on the programme as well as Freddie Randall and his band.

In 1959 Jack appeared on the BBC Guitar Club broadcast from Bristol. The producer John Kingdon offered Jack more work on Guitar Club and this led to an association with the violinist Leslie Baker and the formation of the Swingtette based on the Hot Club of France Quintet, which did three thirteen week series on the BBC late night show "Stringalong" (10.30pm to midnight). Further broadcasts followed. Jack had several thirteen week contracts with the "Late Live Show" (midnight to 2am), when listeners would phone in with requests. The Jack Toogood Quartet with Bristol pianist Alan Hurley featured in several programmes from the West Region, such as "Rhythm Rendezvous", "Tap your Feet" and "Spotlight on the Jack Toogood Quartet". The J T Q's signature tune was "Lullaby of the Leaves" with which they played the programme in and out.

Jack had no recordings of these "Late Live Show" broadcasts, but a fan in Walton-on-Thames taped the programmes on reel to reel recorder from his radio and passed them on to Jack, who now has them on cassette. Obviously the reproduction is not all that good, but it does give a flavour of the fine music produced by the band. What is difficult now to take seriously is the BBC style of announcing,(particularly the West of England Broadcasts), the incredibly plummy, over the top accent now seems so stilted.

Jack, with Colin Hawke on bass also backed Jimmy Young, playing piano and vocals on several BBC recordings including "Too Young" on TV. There were other TV appearances, "Looking for the Stars" on TWW, the forerunner of HTV, and "Stanorama" on HTV, featuring the comedian Stan Stennett, and singer Sammi Brown (aka Chris Staples),later a member of Sweet Substitute.

Jack recalled musicians that he regularly played with: Johnnie Van Derrick, violin; Alan Metcalf, rhythm guitar; Peter Collins, bass, and Denny Piercy, drums. Jack has played with many bands, more recently with Groove Juice Special and Sweet Substitute and, back with two long time friends and colleagues, Don Burnell and Les Drake in John Watson's Dukes of Swing, where they played the style of music Jack has been most associated with.

In his music room at his home, full of interesting records, tapes, sheet-music etc, is a collection of stringed instruments: ukukle-banjos, cello and round hole guiters, and among them a little ukulele, but not the one I was told that got him 'going' on guitar. There is also an interesting photograph, which on closer inspection is a collage/composition of Jack, Eddie Lang, Django Reinhardt and Charlie Christian, Jack's heroes of the guitar.

Editor's interview with Jack Toogood

Jack, gracing the cover of the BMG magazine (Banjo, Mandolin and Guitar), January 1962. He bought his first copy of this publication in January 1940.

THE ITALIAN CONNECTION

MICHAEL (Mike) WATSON

My Mother was a fine pianist so it is not surprising that I was introduced to music at an early age. I became a boy singer and soloist, and learned to play the banjo ukulele at the age of 7/8 years. The plectrum guitar caught my interest at about 10 years, when I studied with Lew Carson and later with Reg Bishop. For a lesson with Reg, which then cost 2s 6d, I used to cycle from Bishopston to Brislington with my guitar case on the handlebars.

The organist at a church where I sang was Hedley Goodall, who was a well-known drama teacher and actor. He became my mentor and at his production of J. M. Barrie's "The Boy David" he picked me to play David to his Saul. It was the success of this play that resulted in my leaving school in 1938 and moving to London to study drama at the L.A.M.D.A. which lead to work in radio, films and the theatre. However, at the outbreak of War, all contracts were cancelled so I returned to Bristol and joined the BBC as a Junior Programme Engineer. There I met Reg Williams and joined his trio, which included Percy Waterhouse, a fine clarinet player. With my totally acoustic guitar, we formed a quartet and played for Saturday night dances at the Victoria Rooms, for which my pay was 10 shillings. Although I had begun broadcasting as a child actor, my first broadcasts on guitar were with that quartet. Life at the BBC during the early part of the War was hectic but interesting, working with many big names in the entertainment business.

In 1942 I joined the Royal Navy, in which I trained as an electrical mechanic. When qualified, I joined H.M.S. Slinger, an escort carrier, which not long afterwards was blown out of the water by an acoustic mine in the North Sea. We were towed to a dry dock at Woolwich. While ashore, I managed to visit Hatchetts in Piccadilly and on occasions sat in with musicians such as Stephane Grapelli and George Shearing. After repairs, the ship sailed to the Far East. A quartet was formed on board with 2 guitars and vocals, and we did some broadcasts in Australia where I met some good musicians and enjoyed playing in Jazz clubs. Later I was transferred to the destroyer H.M.S. Urania which joined the Pacific Fleet. After the surrender we were involved with occupational duties in Japan, where I once played with a dance band, but at that time did not feel they had quite got the hang of things. I was lucky to remain unscathed for the whole of the War.

After de-mob in 1946 I re-joined the BBC but things were not the same. Having at short notice to organise a recording on, say, farming at 9pm, could get in the way of a pre-arranged gig, so in 1948 I resigned to free-lance as an actor and musician. From 1948 to 1968 I played Sid Luscombe in the West Region radio family serial, "The Luscombes". I also began studying Spanish/classical guitar, having been inspired after listening to Segovia on the radio. Practice on this instrument filled all my free time after my commitments and other activities.

I recall playing with Johnny Bristow (piano) and Ken Trott (bass) in the restaurant of the Grand Hotel for their dinner dances. When a band was formed at the Grand Spa Hotel (now the Avon Gorge Hotel), Johnny Bristow and I were augmented by Don Burnell (sax/clari/flute), Ken Morgan (drums), and my dear friend Colin Hawke (bass). Others during that period and into the 1950s were Les Drake (piano), Laurie Davis (violin/sax), Basil Sharp (drums) and Ken Trott (bass). Bigger bands were introduced at the Grand Spa under Teddy White and John Roberts, in which I was involved.

Sitting in a dance band night after night can lose its fascination. So in 1954 I left and took a gamble in founding the

A publicity photograph taken in the early 1950's by Studio Shergold.

Spanish Guitar Centre, principally for teaching. It meant a lot of hard work but the gamble paid off. In 1955 I studied at the Summer School held at Accademia Chigiana, Sienna. It was there that I renewed by friendship with John Williams, the classical guitarist. Pupil numbers at the Centre grew and it became necessary to enlist help from the best pupils. Gordon Saunders was one of these, and eventually he became a partner, helping considerably with teaching and building the commercial side of the business. At one time 3 of us were teaching about 240 pupils a week, giving private and class tuition. Among my talented pupils were Anthea Gifford, who became a world-class player. I recall sending her to Sienna to study under Alisio Diaz, where she was awarded one of the rare scholarships. Louise Durrent, another fine player was my duet partner in a classical guitar duo. Over the years the Centre developed to be known nationally and internationally.

Back in 1948 Duncan Wood produced a series of Folk Dance programmes with members of the English Folk Song & Dance Society Band from London, augmented by Colin Hawke, Don Burnell, Ken Morgan and me as the Bristol contingent. Esme Lewis, a fine singer from Wales, was a guest at one show. Later I became her accompanist and recorded with her. She introduced me to TWW (later, HTV) in Cardiff. For many years I worked on shows, playing both classic guitar and the jazz box, including work with the BBC there. We had a fine quintet composed of Brian Short or Colin Hawke (bass), Roy Herbert (accordionist), Jonny Dean (drums), and Tony Arnopp (sax/clari/flute) - (these 2 both London session musicians). Eddie Clayton would have joined us had the shows not clashed with his resident commitments with the Ashton Court Country Club. These contacts in Cardiff were to prove most helpful to me for many years.

Although the Spanish Guitar Centre was occupying most of my time I also managed the odd recital and TV work. It was a pretty power packed time, none of which I would have missed as I have so many happy memories. One is of some great jazz sessions at the White Hart in Lower Ashley Road with names (forgotten by some) such as Les Drake (piano), Bill Turner (sax), Sid Uppington (bass), Don Burnell (sax), and Paul Brodie (drums). Boy, did we blow up a storm! And without mics or amps!! It is a pity those days seem to have gone.

Another memory is of enjoying some musical fun in a little

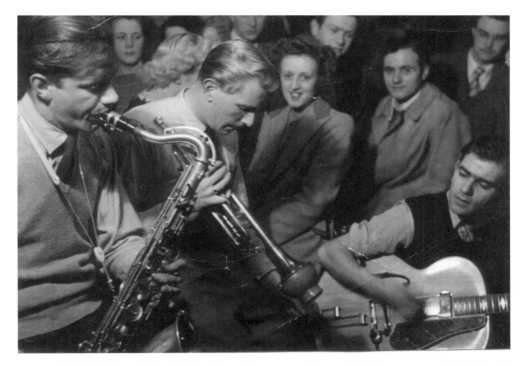

An early 1950's photo of, L to R: Don Burnell, tenor sax; Duncan Wood, trumpet, and Mike Watson, guitar. Also playing in the group, but out of picture were: Les Drake, piano; Bill Turner, sax; Sid Uppington, bass, and Paul Brodie, drums. This was an informal, but regular get together for musicians and the band had no name. Photo taken at the White Hart in Lower Ashley Road.

drinking club in Clifton in the mid 50s with Geoff Weldrake (bass) and John Nixon, who played sax and, would you believe, some great jazz on a concertina. More recently, I was privileged to have the guitar chair in the Roger Lawdon band, Bristol Cream. His death was a sad loss to music locally.

When retirement beckoned I handed over the reins of the S.G.C. to Chris Gilbert, who carries on in different premises, now in Coldharbour Road. Since then, I have enjoyed sessions with my musical friends. I am grateful to Graham Leavey who has engaged me on gigs; and Jack Ashton, who

must also be mentioned for his valiant work in keeping music alive in Bristol. It is impossible to mention, or even remember, all the musicians which whom I have been fortunate enough to work over the years.

Mike Watson

115

BRISTOL JAZZ, MY PART IN MY DOWNFALL

Q WILLIAMS

I've been trying to play Boogie-Woogie since schooldays, from about 1944/5 onwards (age 13 or so), having been dazzled by recordings of Frankie Carl, Harry James and then the 1947 movie "The Hucksters". I was at school with Geoff Nichols where, when we were about 14 or 15, he astounded us all with his drumming skill. It came as a big surprise to me about 1944 when I realised that what he really wanted to do was to play the trumpet. Previous to this I had no idea there were trumpeters in jazzbands: I had only seen a caricature of Louis Armstrong by Sheriff in "Punch". I went to the Arcade in Broadmead with Geoff about 1945 to buy his first trumpet. It cost £3 -15s- 0d, if I remember rightly. (Because I can remember this kind of thing, and he can't, he's nowadays accusing me of re-inventing his past.) In those days we listened to Ladnier, Bechet, Keppard and everybody else really, including the very shocking (for those days) Cab Calloway. It turns out, of course, that who Geoff was really interested in was Louis Armstrong.

Geoff, Cliff Brown, Brian Rushton and myself met one sunny Saturday in Geoff's parent's house in Ashley Down to play some 'first steps' jazz. Geoff was on trumpet, Brian on trombone, Cliff on clarinet and myself on drums - an old kit of Cliff's. From that moment on, in about 1946, I was, and have always been, daunted by the whole business. It became for me a kind of exalted world of especially difficult performance technology. It's successful exponents (the local Blue Star Quintet, Arthur Parkman, Tony Mogford and Co.) seemed to me to be not so much gods as some sort of tech-whiz boffins who had surrounded themselves with an elite threshold of high-tech competence. The world stars were of course, out of this world. That afternoon was a failure. Brian knew a few licks and floated them out into the middle of the room with doubtful relevance. Cliff, whose clarinet playing was only rudimentary, spent most of the session correcting my drumming, and Geoff was left to pick the bones out of the mess. Incidentally, I've listened to both drummers comparatively recently and Cliff remains the closest in feeling to Baby Dodds. And whatever you think of Baby Dodds, he surprises me every time I hear him.

In September 1948 I went to Art School and began to think about leaving it all behind me, becoming interested instead in Caravaggio and Feliks Topolski. I still nagged at the old college canteen piano and our old clapped-out crate at home but really wasn't into it, apart from making sure, out of vanity, that Geoff and I played a duo piano and drums cabaret at our first Christmas Arts Ball. Geoff was a trainee blood technician at Southmead Hospital for a day job. We went as Anglo-Indians in turbans and seersucker suits. John E. Jones, the darling of the painting school announced us. I admired his good order, leaving our names till last."On piano and drums", he bellowed...... " Williams and Nichols!!" I was still very diffident and shy of the hard engineering brilliance of, for example, a drum kit or the bewildering plumbing of a tenor saxophone, and I was still playing the piano mainly in F sharp, the black keys...it seemed simpler.

Three musical projects invaded my life between 1948, when I started at Art School, and 1954, when I left. (I was there such a long time because I failed two exams - maybe I "fool at that piano too much".) Geoff and I and pianist Gordon Redman formed a small band called Gordon Redman's Wolverines in about 1949/50. There were four of us including Brian Rushton and I suppose two or three church-hall dances wasn't bad for a band in which the bass player (me)

Portrait photo of Q, courtesy of H.M. Passport Office.

didn't have a clue what he was doing. The ensemble folded decently quickly. Geoff played for a while in something probably quite successful as a dance band called Ron Winter's Rhythm Group. Round about this time he and I played at the Redcliffe Street Jazz Club. He played "Stormy Weather" and I sang "Alexander's Ragtime Band" but I honestly can't remember whether I was playing piano or bass, or nothing at all, just singing. Perhaps I was holding a tin cup.

Then Geoff left Ron Winters because he'd met some blokes who were keen to do the real stuff. Pete Conibear's mother kept a dress shop called "Eunice" in Redcliffe Hill. One Saturday afternoon in 1949 I went with Geoff up to the top floor of this terraced establishment to witness the first encounter of those cats who turned out to be the first Avon Cities Jazz Band - G. Nichols, trumpet; Ray (Butch) Bush, clarinet; Pete Conibear, alto-sax; Conrad (Dizzie) Gillespie, trombone; Johnny Macey, banjo and I think Jay Hawkins, banjo - but I may be wrong, no drums (but again I may be wrong). Also there was no piano. Geoff at this time

seemed to think I was going eventually to play the piano properly - it was only a matter of time, etc., but I never really got around to it in the way he meant. Anyway he seemed, at that point keen to be saying I was going to be the piano man. But he didn't keep this up for long, and quite right too. Glyn Wilcox turned out to be their first pianist. I had quailed again and disappeared once more into fine art.

In 1950, Gloucester Road, one of Bristol's most successful shopping centres, was like a football crowd. You trogged from one shop to the next at snail's pace, elbowing people out of the way, hoping for a pair of cords or a shirt or a '78' of Bessie Smith you could afford. I met Cliff Brown there one Saturday afternoon. He said he'd been drumming for a bunch of cats at Pensford...and why didn't I come down as they didn't have a pianist? "But", I said, "I can only play in F sharp". "That", said Cliff "doesn't matter". I thought it mattered enormously but didn't like to argue.

The first rehearsal I attended, of what became Acker Bilk's Chew Valley Jazz Band was held in the Miners' Welfare Hall in Pensford in 1950/51. Acker was on clarinet, John Skuse on trombone, self on piano, Roy King on banjo, Mike Redstone on a soap-box bass and Cliff on drums. Our dire need was a trumpet player but we managed to straighten out a few important principles just at that first meeting. I wouldn't say Acker was autocratic but because he knew, and could do, more music than the rest of us, we generally did what he wanted and it worked quite well.

The Pensford practices continued on Tuesday evenings and Sunday afternoons and we began to play engagements. We did a sort of variety concert in Filton Parish Hall and a dance at the RAF camp at South Cerney, another at RAF Lyneham and a village dance at Chew Magna. By now Joe Brickell, the Bath trumpet player hadn't joined the band but the cornettist John Hill of Cheddar had. John could put notes in the air - place them rather than blow them - a lot like Bix. I must confess that I took Acker's playing for granted rather than listened to it attentively, and I reckon that started by my being so concerned with the validity, or otherwise, of my own playing. I was of course playing in F, C, G, B flat and so on by then, with, as Acker likes to remember it, his fist under my ear. After the South Cerney RAF gig Cliff said to me, "You're rattling it out now" which I took as a compliment and encouragement.

I had by the early 1950s begun to compose ragtime pieces for the piano. During those early days I ventured to coach some Art School contemporaries of mine in the art of Jazz Band and actually played the trombone a couple of times in public in 1952/3. Where did I get such brass neck? Also I made a recording on piano of "Going Home" (after Ken Colyer, not Dvorak), "Frankie and Johnny" and "Over there in Gloryland" with the late Roger Baker, guitar and vocals and Brian Huggett on clarinet.

We shall draw a discreet veil over those proceedings except to say that this little combo was entitled The Rave-Cravers Sciffle Group -(That's right-sciffle with a "c") and that my friend Geoff Ogilvie, on hearing this dire effort said "Keerist, it sounds like a séance!!" By this time the Avons, of course, were playing all over the place and recording quite decent stuff like "Moose March" and the "Notre-Dame Football Anthem", "Tiger Rag" and so forth. Acker's band hotted up - people came and went. By 1953 John Hill had been replaced on trumpet by John Stainer, an engineering student from the London area. John was a real tonic. It needs another book to tell sufficiently funnily of his exploits. Mike Redston was replaced on bass by Brian Walker on tuba and then Chick Martin and /or Sandy Miller back on bass. Mike Braund, from our Art School band replaced Cliff Brown on drums.

The Cassey Bottom band from Hanham emerged, merged onto and into the music scene at this time, about 1953-5, and a kind of more open pattern, rather than system, of musical camaraderie was prevalent at the Crown and Dove - a wonderful old style 'Order-of-Buffaloes-and-mirrors-all-round-the -walls' sort of establishment opposite the Fire Station at the Horsefair. Among the patrons were Dave and Jean Hibberd, Billy Bilk, Zank Sawyer, John and Jenny Gully, Peter O'Toole, Margaret Morris, T.K.Daniel, Chris Penny,

Adge Cutler, Ogle, Pete and Marge Kemp and so on.

Brian Savegar from Cardiff, whose dapper obsession with well-cut suits earned him Ann Collett's sobriquet "the original Welsh Dresser", joined Acker's band on trumpet and various people came up on tour from London and points east, and a more cross-country feeling began round and about. The band members were Acker, clarinet; Brian Savegar, trumpet; John Stainer, trumpet; John Skuse, trombone; self, piano; Cliff Brown, drums; Mike Braund, drums; Sandy Miller, bass; Michael Worms and Jay Hawkins, banjos.

The Avons, beginning to be successful more widely about now, were falling prey to a strange sort of insularity which has intrigued and amused me for many years. The band consisted of Geoff Nichols, trumpet; Jan Ridd, piano; (Butch) Bush, clarinet; Basil Wright, drums; (Dizzy) Gillespie, trombone; Malcolm Wright, bass; Mike Hitchings, clarinet; Johnny Macey and Jay Hawkins, banjos.

During these early times, 1950-55 or so, the Avons played every Friday evening in the tennis pavilion of the YWCA building at the top of Great George Street and were building a steady reputation and following in Bristol, and in other parts of the country. When the founder member and clarinettist (Butch) Bush took over the management from the firm footing achieved by T.K. Daniel, and then much more seriously by Mike Bevan, it's safe to say that the Avons became tantamount to a professional band. Members were paid for attending rehearsals and engagement fees were comparable with those of professional bands. Recordings proliferated on the market. Butch was, and still is, a hustler. But when you're as successful as that you become very busy, and you sometimes don't have time to pay attention to everything else that's going on around you. Many times over the last thirty years I've seen surprise on the faces of Avon's founder members when confronted by the achievements of others in the field which they'd been too busy to know about. The most classic example of this was in the late eighties when Dave Collett, Chris Pope, and with, I think Clive Morton on bass, working as a trio, Howlin' Winds out of the Avons, did a broadcast from the

White Hart in Park Row, with Butch who was on a return visit from California. I said to Dave that I'd been unaware of his trio's connection with the White Hart. "We've been playing there for a few weeks", he replied, "but what d'you expect when you've got talent?" (Shyly proud). It was a mark of my increasing maturity of demeanour (I was then aged about 57) that I forbore to mention that I myself had been playing there with my quartet for nearly two and a half years viz.; self, on piano; Dave Hibberd on drums, Dave Griffiths on bass, and Geoff Nichols on trumpet and vibes. Mike Watson joined us later on guitar. It is highly unlikely you see that word about us at the White Hart had reached the Avons even though one of them, the leader, had been playing there for more than two years in my quartet. More of this later, but when Butch sent me over a talking tape of his American exploits in 1990, he still didn't know Howlin' Winds hadn't been first at the White Hart! All of this reads, of course, like small-minded professional jealousy, but I only intended it to be a comment on professional isolationism. We're all a bit long in the tooth now for jealousy. Dave Collett looks back on the early days of alleged rivalry between Acker's band and the Avons with affectionate amusement. "WE hated each other's guts," he says, "despite the fact we'd never met, and didn't know the first thing about each other".

Back to 1950 for a moment: John Stainer and I had to wait at Pensford for the Bristol bus late one Sunday afternoon. Fortunately the bus stop was close enough to the Miners' Hall for us to hear Acker and Roy King, on banjo, playing the coal fire out with about fifty choruses of "Shine". The bus was a long time coming. I feel, retrospectively, very privileged to have heard this deep cornucopia of improvisatory ideas played by the master, as if for our special benefit. The invention was endless, like in a Buddy Rich extended solo feature, or a show by Victor Borge - outstanding, possibly even 'great.'

On the 4th of August 1954 I was due to report to the army depot in Exeter, Royal Electrical and Mechanical Engineers - Engineers? - Me? Even nowadays I'm still struggling with scissors. What it meant was - I left Acker's Chew Valley Jazz Band and went into the army, and Dave Collett took over

from me. Dave says the real reason for my leaving the band was that my steady girlfriend of those days was jealous of it and I was trying to keep her sweet. Well if that's the case I failed to do that from Honiton, Plymouth, Beaconsfield and Ripon, and when I was demobbed 2 years later we were both married to somebody else.(that's me and the girl of course, not me and Dave).

Now comes the bit about Acker taking the Band down to London to try to crash the big time. First of all it became the Paramount Jazz Band and went to tour Poland. Roy Smith was on drums now, Jay Hawkins, late of the Avons, on banjo, Johnny Macey on bass, Dave Collett on piano, Ack on clarinet, John Stainer on trumpet and John Skuse on trombone. It was Poland's first sniff for many years of western decadence and they were hosing ticket crashers off the roofs of the Sportsplatz in Krakov and Gdansk. Then, as I understand it, double ignominy set in. After a short time in London during which everybody was more than cheesed off, including Acker himself (he wrote me a letter from "22 Bloody Lillie Road, Brompton"), the boys in the band filtered back to Bristol and resumed their day jobs and local gigs. What is really depressing, however, is that the boys in Acker's new Paramount Jazz Band, London based boys that is, also had day jobs - at first. What a pity it is, isn't it, that the self-same capability condition of half a dozen blokes is eminently susceptible to improvement in one town but not in another just 100 miles away? Mike Bevan's and Butch's job on promoting the Avons has been exemplary, and the music itself has been so-called 'world class'. But because we have such scandalous cultural centralism in this country it's still Humph, Barber, Stan Tracey and the rest of the 'Londits'remaining in the forefront.

I got a little band together in the army... surprising what a rank and 'class' leveller jazz is. We had privates, sergeants and captains in our little band. The trumpet player was Chris Pemsell. He wasn't in the mob at all but his father was principal of Harrogate Art School and so we met up at evening classes there - Chris is a TV producer now. You may recall his art direction on "The Barchester Chronicles".

The Oriole Band at the Regency Ballroom, Bath, about 1960. L to R: Terry Fry, Q Williams, John Stainer, Nick Cooper, Sandy Miller, Gordon Mogridge and Geoff Over.

Those years 1952-57, say, are a bit hazy. It is hard to name the bands in Bristol at this time - much more easy to remember the musicians. The transition from the activities of members of the Avons, Chew Valley, Cassey Bottom and Bath based bands to the formation of the Oriole Jazz Band was diffuse and ragged in the memory.

Adge Cutler is remembered at the Crown and Dove singing, with Acker's band, numbers like "Drink up Thee Cider" and "Scrumpy-Drinkin' Brickies from Home"(a parody of "Cakewalking Babies"). I have drawings I did of Acker, John

Stainer and John Skuse playing at the Crown and Dove and also of Michel Worms (Brackets-French) and Roy King on guitars. Apply to this author for alarming anecdotes about Michel. I remember a New Year's dance at the Crown and Dove which finished at 10.30p.m.due to an unbelievably extensive fight between about eighty people who, three seconds beforehand had been merrily dancing. Or else that was the evening when a couple of young ladies tried to push each other's heads in the fire. Nothing much changes except the technology, I suppose. Images of John Skuse and John Stainer come and go. Mike Braund the drummer went off to Market

Drayton. Nev. Finch, a banjo player from somewhere up north, came and went. Chick Martin and Brian Savegar melted away, also a little valve trombone player from Cardiff, whose name always escapes me.

Dave Collett and John Stainer formed the Stainer /Collett 7-Phoenix out of Acker's ashes. Keith Box and Reg Quantrill got me on piano so I must have played 'for a quid or so' in either Keith Box' Cassey Bottom band or else the Keith Box Jazzmen - I can't clearly remember. Anyway, it was like this: Terry Fry (Harry-cum-Lauder of St. George Grammar School) was first and only trombonist with the Oriole Jazz Band of Bristol. What trouble he caused by leaving his Cassey Bottom connections I don't know? Nick Cooper, like me a Sea Mills man, with, unlike me, an incisive and relentless approach to his instrument was our clarinettist. Mike Tyzack, of Clowne in Derbyshire, then either at Slade School of Art in London, or teaching at Cardiff Art School, led us on trumpet. There are two recording sessions by this band - one of them,a BBC radio session, appears to be lost- contact me if you have it).

Geoff Nichols, hearing Mike Tyzack on these old tapes, doesn't rate him. He's wrong. Mike was in those days a quiet, red-hot trumpet lead. I suppose he had to be with Nick blowing all round him like a storm. A lesser man would have passed out. Terry Fry was the most tuneful of trombonists. His solos sounded not much different from his backing but I could always forgive that because his backing was so exemplary. Gordon Mogridge was a hard - driving drummer who swept us all along with him. Gareth (Boots) Griffiths played banjo and, for some completely unnecessary reason, was replaced, by Geoff Over, who was then in the RAF and now plays in the Mike Daniels Band.

Sandy Miller was an old stager: a perky cockney who lived in Cotham and worked as secretary to "His Excellency the Governor of Horfield Prison." Sandy played a bouncing tone on the bass - no clicks or slaps - and had immense confidence in himself as a street fighter, despite being, quite honestly, a 7-stone weakling. Sandy always drank a pint of cold water before retiring after his customary several pints of beer during the evening out. I can't imagine many evenings of his being evenings in. Anyway, we came second in the N.F.J.O. competition of 1953. We went to Birmingham for the honour and had sausage sandwiches at New Street station afterwards. I can't remember the name of the winning band. It was a modern combo of some kind: I remember being impressed by the drummer, a dapper chap flapping the traps like billy-oh.

When I came out of the army I played for a while with the Keith Box band, then disappeared into married and domestic and working life and started bringing up some children.

In 1964 I appeared on Acker Bilk's "This is Your Life" (and was amazed to discover how (a) sycophancy is almost an industry wherever 'celebrity' occurs, (b) That Eammon Andrews was a very nice man, (c) that 'Professor' Stanley Unwin speaks deconstructed English all the time, and (d) that George Lewis was there from New Orleans and had no white hair at all - or else it was tinted.

In 1964 I was in the first Henry's Bootblacks LP "Vintage Jazz" at the Ship Inn. Henry Davies, bass; self, piano; John Hallier, drums; (Boots) Griffiths, banjo/guitar; David Emmett and Dick Farler, trumpets; Brian Mann, Jim Osborne and Nick Cooper, reeds; Terry Fry, Ron Brown, trombones. A stomp orchestra in the early Ellington mould: "Copenhagen", "The Mooch", "Black and Tan Fantasy". We split down into a 7 piece for Morton numbers: "Black Bottom Stomp", "The Chant", "Smoke-house Blues" -thrilling. We played mostly at the Ship Inn in Redcliffe Hill to a large and appreciative following.

This (1964) was the year the Blue Notes were playing at the Ship, and also, I think, (Spooks) Radford and Kloop Cox with their boppercombo. The Ship, I believe, had more authentic atmosphere than anywhere else in town - but it was hard competition , apart, that is, from the nearly total absence of black faces on the scene at the time. Champion Jack Dupree guested with us one night. He told me he was, at that time, living in Switzerland. He said, "We skis, us Swiss". You'll have to ask John Stainer or somebody about the American guests at the Crown and Dove - Wild Bill, Sonny Terry, Brownie McGhee and so on: I was either in the army or off the scene.

John Hallier and I were buzzed out of the Bootblacks. I packed it all in for a while, until 1967 in fact, when Cliff Brown and Barry Back, a colleague of his at the Bristol Film Unit, persuaded me to join a comedy trio called The Alligator Jug Thumpers and go on the road with Adge Cutler's Wurzels. Adge had been developing his comedy music steadily and was working with the late Norman Beaton, the Dewar Brothers, Adrienne Webber and Derek Brimstone. The folk scene had arrived. By this time I had received very early warning of the Beatles (from an article in Scene - remember "Scene"?) - it only lasted a few months and seemed endlessly concerned with the career of Robert Mitchum and had discovered Bob Dylan. He sat on the stairs in a play on BBC black-and-white TV called "Mad House on Butcher Street" and played his poetic stuff. I was entranced. I said to our lodger,Michael Ainsleigh-Thomas, "Watch out for this guy. If he's not going to be a success, no one is!" Dylan was 16 then. No one had ever heard of him - and he certainly didn't look anything like he did later on.

The Alligator Band wowed them on tour: Torquay, Taunton, Plymouth and so on, but oddly,we never recorded until well into the seventies, when we were re-formed to do a number in a BBC film with Neil Innes from the Bonzo Dog Band, "Sweet Miss Emmalina".

I met Bill Brown in the early seventies and I also went on tour with Stephane Grappelli. I'll say about Grappelli first. Reg Mann, a dairy manager with some money put by, got to promoting some tours starring Stephane with the Diz Disley Trio: Diz and Ike Isaacs with Len Skeat on bass. We did Bristol, Exeter, Barnstaple, Taunton, Camborne and Plymouth. Talk about stage fright. The Colston Hall with Grappelli was a bit different from appearing with the Adge Cutler Show and the Alligator Jug Band. The butterflies in one's stomach were actually vampire bats. I was the warm-up, playing some of my original ragtime pieces on all the concert grands in the South West. Grappelli was polite. He was always surprised to see me still there before every show. He would say, "air you playing again toonight? Zat's good because zen I can 'ave extra little ress before the consair aftair deenair". So that's me as a jazz performer folks - Grappelli's bismuth.

The Camborne gig was the funniest. There was a bloke up a ladder fixing the lights well into my third number and the piano had been painted. It would have been better painted shut.

An old battle-axe of a county-set matron buttonholed Grappelli in the dressing room at Plymouth and demanded to know, in my hearing, why I was necessary to the show. Grappelli wasn't a real trouper in my opinion. A tad over-aware of his own genius and a musical bromide in a sense; always keen to point out to potential rivals how difficult it is to play the violin. I don't know if he ever did any teaching, but if so, I should think his pupils would have been made quickly suicidal. Anyway, on this occasion, despite the fact that he had known the old bat in Devon during the war, Grappelli just gave her a gallic shrug in answer to her nasty question and thereby, I suppose, tacitly invited her to supply her own answer. Len Skeat, throughout, looked disapproving of everything and Diz and Ike were very friendly and supportive. I got to play with Diz several times after that, in pubs in Bristol and Bath and once at my home at a party.

Bill Brown was an American intellectual from San Francisco. Tall, athletically built, a fortunate physical mixture of everything good in the Celtic/Anglo-Saxon physique. He always reminded me of a rugged edition of Orson Welles. His choice of reading matter used to give me a touch of the Tony Hancocks after one and a half sentences. He could speak several languages including Japanese and, as a young artist in 'Frisco before coming here, he had begun to make a name for himself as a painter. I've seen photographs of these early works and they struck me as the acme/epitome of artistic synergy. I've never elsewhere seen such panache-as if he were trying for a whole painting with one glory-stroke of the brush.

His later pictures, in Portugal and Bristol, were very different - still dazzlingly bright but now much more slow and meticulous. His approach to the trumpet was extremely methodical.

I met him first at the Bristol Flyer where his band was playing a one-off evening in 1972. I can't remember the name of the band - it was before his Swing-Shift, I think. But anyway it had Bill on cornet and flugel horn, Bernie Newland on trombone, Dennis Harris on banjo and Pete Hunt on bass. I can't remember the other cats. With Bill it was the joy of musical experiment and experience. The name of the band didn't matter. Those years of the early 70s are even dimmer for me than all the rest. I remember playing with Bill's band in Weston-Super-Mare, with Eddie Lomax on alto, at various private functions and at the Old Duke, by which time, I suppose, it must have been called Swing-Shift.

Bernie Newland, erstwhile trombonist of the Mike Daniel's band, who had just become a widower, left his home in Wellington and came to live with Joan and I in 1975 to take part in the jazz scene. Bernie, like many Londoners, while being well able and willing to take advice, was over-enthusiastic about dishing it out and was not universally popular. He died a couple of years ago in Germany, where he lived with his new wife, Annegret. I miss him sorely and we sometimes go to visit Annegret and she comes here.

I count it as a privilege that Toni, Bill Brown's widow, asked me to write the British end of a brochure blurb for his San Francisco posthumous retrospective exhibition a few years ago. Bill died in 1980, much too early, he was just fifty years of age. I was devastated. He had been involved more and more in his Big Band - a 14 piece swing and stomp orchestra, more or less under the direction of Bill and the guitarist Jim Jenkins. It's been done before but I remember being very impressed by Bill's method of working out chords (for horns) with exceptionally wide intervals. It was a slat of wood as precisely long as the piano keyboard, with clothes pegs to be placed and altered at the requisite positions across the registration. Bill was always at the scene, either playing, arranging, listening, and sitting in on a big bongo drum he took to

lugging about. We did a completely unrehearsed and wild gig at the Granary at about this time. I got together a 14-piece band and we played all we knew and got paid quite well. I remember the guitarist Johnny Viner being highly amused at the instalments of money I kept giving him. There was a big thrash of in-memoriam celebration of Bill's life when he died. The guitarist Pete Hull got very angry about not being asked to play. Quite right too. He'd been in Swing-Shift after all. I can't remember how responsible I thought I should have been for this.

Tony Osborne, the trumpet player in Gerry Bath's Climax Jazz Band in the 50s, came back to live in Bristol in 1975. He'd been away for 18 years, teaching in London. Strolling into the Duke one night he was quite taken by one or two cats in whatever band it was that night, who, without blinking, said "Ullo Tone, want a blow?" They'd been, he supposed, vaguely aware he'd been away somewhere for a couple of weeks.

About 1975 I got a band together with Tony McCarthy. We called it McQ. Rehearsals were awful. I spent them fuming at everyone else's knackered and sporadic attention to why we were there. When Tony McCarthy left we got Richard Thomas in on drums and called it Q6, since it was a sextet. We did a TV show and interview by A.C.H. Smith. We also did a fantastic film at the BBC studios in Whiteladies Road. It was the most swashbuckling, panache-bedecked movie I've ever seen about anything, let alone jazz. Kate McNab, tonsils; Bernie Newland, trombone; Dave Kingston, trumpet; Clive Taylor, clarinet; self on piano; Dave Pyne, bass, and Dickie Thomas, drums. But the apathy about rehearsals persisted (and still does to this day) and I finally folded the band.

Then began one of the more enjoyable and leisurely times of my musical life, such as it's been. I went down the Old Duke and said to John Stone, "Look here, I've done a lot of work here at the Old Duke when Kon and Alma Aniol were here. I reckon you ought to let me have a regular gig if I pick a good band,and believe me, I'm not going to inflict a bad one on you, for all our sakes". It was agreed, then, that Q's Company, as Dave Hibberd named it, would play at the Old Duke about 3 or 4 times a year. I'll get around to the details directly but must first mention that, just before this, I'd organised a band at the Flyer in Gloucester Road called The Ifical Moon Band: Roger Wells, drums; Brian Halliwell, guitar; Spud Taylor, bass; self, piano; Nick Cooper, reeds; Tony Osborne, trombone, and 'handsome' Hugh Hillier on trumpet. Hoppy Hopkins sometimes played instead of Tony because, I think, of Tony's Blue Notes and other commitments. Also, Dave Collett and I after too long a time hanging about, finally put together a 2-piece piano Boogie-Woogie LP called "Back to Boogie-Woogie". This LP, despite it's mediocre commercial degree of success, (because, of course, it was produced in 'the regions') is probably the most precisely and tightly played Boogie-Woogie collection ever made. It's certainly the most innovative. The LP was reviewed on Radio Bristol and Derek Robinson on HTV.

But to get back to the heady days at the Old Duke and to Q's Company. The band was/is basically Dave Hibberd, drums; self, piano; Dave Griffiths, Clive Morton, 'smooth' Maurice Everson or Cas Caswell, bass; Frank Feeny or Mike Watson, guitar; Geoff Nichols, trumpet; Tony Osborne, trombone; Frank Fennell, Andy Leggett, Chris Pearce, John Barton and (now sadly) the late Mike Ludlow, reeds.

Danny Moss, Jeannie Lamb, Dennis Armstrong, Acker Bilk and Roy Williams have guested and sat in, and we've had some real wall-to-wall moving experiences down the Duke.

About the White Hart, it goes like this: the landlord of the White Hart in Park Row was a very nice man with a very serious heart condition who was totally loco about jazz music and whose name has completely escaped me. I played him a cassette of one of our Old Duke sessions, the one with Roy Williams on it, and we were in. It was my gig, therefore we played as, I think, Q4, a quartet. What I am absolutely certain about however, is that (a) it wasn't called Good Vibes, even if Geoff Nichols took it elsewhere under that name with a different pianist - and (b) that it was at the White Hart two and a half years before Howlin' Winds(but perhaps me do protest too much).

In 1993 Acker, Roy King, Brian Walker, Jay Hawkins, Johnny Hill, John Skuse and Cliff Brown and I went down to the village hall in Hinton Blewett and made a cassette to commemorate our 40th anniversary.

Nowadays I'm slowly getting all my piano rags transcribed into notation by pianist Carole Penhorwood, and playing the odd gig here and there. Q's Company, plus Acker, did a TV show on behalf of the survival of the Old Duke. Ack, Dave Collett, Roy Smith, Jay Hawkins and I, with our artist friend Ken Leech, sometimes go out drawing and painting en-plein-air.

Bristol musicians can't play quietly enough to be able to listen to each other and have the nonsensical habit of playing backing/riffs in front of, instead of behind solos. They've also lost the knack of the solo or ensemble break, a device capable of endless variation. They also overdo 'fours with the drums' and other clichés. They also think they're too accomplished to bother with rehearsals (this may be why jazz seems, now, to be in the doldrums).

Many fine musicians are now dead: Bill Brown, Ian (Flurge) Appleyard, Terry Fry, Sandy Miller, Trevor Bricker, Eddie Lomax, Bernie Newland, Robin Wood the tuba player, Robin Wood the pianist, Bob Jones, Enoch Hunt the tuba player, Les Drake, Don Burnell, Mike Ludlow, and so it goes on-or does it go on? Ralph Laing reckons it might be all over. Bristol Jazz, any Jazz, all Jazz, is it now the end of a 100 year epoch?

BUT...as Mr Bilk once said to me, *"There will always be someone listening to Dodd's man!"*

Bristol Jazz - my part in my downfall (I can't really blame anybody else).

Q. Williams

A TRIBUTE TO DAVE HIBBERD

I first met Dave Hibberd in the late 1950s. This was at the Ship on Redcliffe Hill and I think he must have started playing drums at about this time. He told me that before he could afford a drum kit he used to drum on the back of a bagatelle board with a friend who played alto sax. This all took place in a shelter in Arnos Court park.

I found out years later that this friend, John Wilkins, was the same man who I met when I began to work in Bath and who started me playing boogie piano. Some coincidence or what?

Dave has retired now because of ill health but was a swinging drummer who worked with numerous bands and small groups during a long career. He was also an excellent singer of ballads and swingers. I worked with him over four decades with the Dave Collett Trio (it should have been the Dave Hibberd Trio really but he was wary of the taxman). We must have played something like 1200 gigs with the Trio with never a cross word and a lot of fun.

I think Dave's great achievement was the concept of this book. Thanks to him the Bristol Jazz Scene has deservedly been documented.

Dave Collett

The beginning of Dave's career, pictured here on the left in 1938, with brothers Roy centre, and Vernon right. They were choirboys at the church of The Holy Nativity, Wells Road.

The George Carver Quartet in the 1970s with left to right, Dave Hibberd, Don Burnell, Maurice West and George Carver.

MORE THAN SKIN DEEP

About DAVE, Drummer, Singer, Compiler, HIBBERD.

When Dave was born with two drums, they were quite useful for listening with but it wasn't until he was about twelve years old that those ear- drums picked up the sound that was to become one of his main reasons for living.

It was during the Big Band era of the 1940s and 50s when the all-important 'wireless' used to bring us the sounds of Oscar Rabin, Lew Stone, Maurice Winnick etc. and as WW2 progressed and the American Forces Network became obligatory listening in our house, the rather more 'punchy' bands like the Dorseys, The Count and The Duke.

I can still hear the exclamations emitting from Dave now as the drummers of those bands made their presence felt with 'flams', 'paradidles' and 'rimshots' so it came about that it was Tommy Dorsey's drummer who made the biggest impact, none other than the late, and arguably the greatest Buddy Rich, who became Dave's role model.

But just to listen was much too passive so he had to look for some sort of equipment that would produce a similar sound. What materialised in fact was an upturned biscuit tin, a few Co-op tin tokens, (does anybody remember? They were the equivalent of your purchase, which were exchanged periodically for dividend if you were a Co-op member with a share number) and to complete the 'kit', a pair of Mother's steel knitting needles, of suitable length of course. A cork was impaled on one end of the needles and these were his primitive but rather effective drum sticks. The Co-op tokens were placed on the tin which, when tapped would produce the sound of a sort of snare drum (using a generous measure of imagination!) Well, everybody has to start somehow and this was an indication of Dave's enthusiasm.

Any thoughts of buying kit were out of the question because in those days church mice were wealthy compared to us. However he persevered with his 'Heath Robinson' set-up until a Sea Cadet mate of mine loaned me a drum kit which he claimed had once been the property of the Bristol variety artist Dump Harris who must have been around the halls before our time. It was a pretty basic kit but it was real and perfectly good enough to get meaningful practice on. So meaningful that Dave and a piano accordionist friend of his entered a talent competition at the Empire Theatre in Old

A publicity card for the Dave Gard Five from the 1970s. Top left Dave Hibberd, top right Ray Winter, bottom left Don Burnell, centre Geoff Weldrake and bottom right Arnold Kanarak.

Dave at The Plough, Bedminster in 1989, where the Dave Collett Trio had a long residency during the 1980s.

Market Street but although their effort failed to score, it's a good indication of the progress that the subject of this article was making.

At some point during the foregoing history, a regimental bass drum was 'acquired' from the local Y.M.C.A. and I seem to remember that Father had a hand in that! Dad was in fact a very modern minded person who was very fond of the music trend of those times so did nothing to discourage number four son in his quest for successful drumnastics. It would be remiss to say the least, not to mention the remarkable good will and wonderful tolerance of our next-door neighbours, who through it all remained quite friendly.

We can only try to imagine the sheer ecstasy eventually that Dave experienced when Buddy Rich brought his own band to Bristol and he was able at long last to sit and watch his idol in the flesh, going through his indescribable performance.

So it came to pass that Dave became part of the Bristol jazz scene and over many years has not only played for many bands around the area but formed some and named some, as the one and only Q. Williams mentioned in Dave's first compilation. I believe the name Q's Company is still retained.

In conversations with jazz followers and musicians where Dave has played, several comments have been made to me bearing testimony to his capability. Blood does not have to be thicker than water for me to agree with those comments that OUR KID is among the best jazz and dance music drummers around the Bristol area and beyond,

P.S. He is some singer too.

Vernon Hibberd.

A New Years Eve celebration at the Old Duke, with left to right Reg Quantrill, John 'Hoppy' Hopkins, Geoff Weldrake, Dave Hibberd and 'Step' Whitehead. Dave was in his element on these occasions and is giving it his all.

CONTRIBUTORS

The editors acknowledge, with warm appreciation, the following, whose co-operation made this book possible.

Tony Beese
Roger Bennett
Mike Bevan
Acker Bilk
Terry Black
Joe Brickell
Ray Bush
Wayne Chandler
Pete Child
Mike Cocks
Jed Collard
Dave Collett
Molly Coombes
Mike Cooper
Bob Coverdale
Dave Creech
Henry Davies
Maurice Everson
Dave Hibberd
Vernon Hibberd
Norman Hill
John Hopkins
Brian Huggett

Nigel Hunt
Alan Hurley
Andy Leggett
Pete Martin
Dave Millman
Geoff Nichols
Brian Osborne
Tony Osborne
Chris Pearce
Chris Pope
Reg Quantrill
Alan Spedding
John Stainer
Mauveen Stone
Jack Toogood
Brian Walker
John Watson
Mike Watson
Geoff Weldrake
Roger Wells
Jill Whittingham
Q Williams

ACKNOWLEDGEMENTS

The editors wish to thank the following for their support, guidance and technical assistance: Geoff, Ian and Margaret Body, Dave Collett and Marcus O'Keefe.

Acknowledgements
Front Cover: Copyright ©Beryl Cook. Reproduced by permission of the artist's family, care of Rogers, Coleridge & White Ltd., 20 Powis Mews, London W11 1JN

(Photographs)
Page 1, from Dave and Jean Hibberd's collection; Page 4, photograph reproduced by kind permission of Marc Marnie, Stagefright Photography; Pages 8 and 12, from Geoff Nichols collection; Pages 13 and 14, photographs by Roy Gallop; Pages 17, 18 and 19, from Roger Bennett's collection; Page 20, from Reg Quantrill's collection; Page 21, photograph reproduced by kind permission of Bromhead Photography; Page 22, from Brian Walker's collection; Page 24, from Nigel Hunt's collection; Pages 26, 27 and 28, from John Stainer's collection; Page 29, from Dave Creech's collection; Page 31, from Dave Collett's collection; Page 33, photograph reproduced by kind permission of John Brewer; Page 34, from Mike Bevan's collection; Pages 37, and 39, from Henry Davies collection; Page 43, from Terry Black's collection; Page 45, from Dave and Jean Hibberds' collection; Page 46, from Mike Cocks collection; Page 49, from Jed Collard's collection; Page 53, from Pete Child's collection; Page 57, from Jill Whittingham's collection; Page 58, from Pete Martin's collection; Page 62, from Brian Osborne's collection; Pages 64 and 65, from John Watson's collection; Page 67, from Alan Spedding's collection; Page 68, from Chris Pope's collection; Page 71, from Andy Leggett's collection; Page 74, from Molly Coombes collection; Pages 76 and 77, from Mike Bevan's collection; Page 80, photograph reproduced by kind permission of Decca Music Group; Page 84, from Andy Leggett's collection; Page 88, photograph from Mike Cock's collection; Page 89, photograph by Roy Gallop; Pages 90 and 91, from Mike Bevan's collection; Page 94, from Mike Bevan's collection; Page 96, from Mike Cocks collection; Page 97, from Maurice Everson's collection; Page 99, from Norman Hill's collection; Page 101, from Brian Huggett's collection; Pages 103 and 104, from June Hurley's collection; Page 106, from Tony Osborne's collection; Page 112, reproduced from cover photograph of B G M magazine; Page 114, photograph, Studios Shergold; Page 115, from Mike Watson's collection; Page 117, from Q Williams collection; Page 120, from Mike Bevan's collection. Page 125-129, from Jean Hibberd's collection.

Many of the photographs reproduced in this book are from the collections of musicians and enthusiasts. Where possible the editors have obtained permission for publication from the photographer or agent. However, in many cases the photographers are unknown or cannot be located. If we have unintentionally infringed copyright we apologise and if informed we will remedy in any subsequent edition.

The editors acknowledge that some of the photographs in this publication are not of the highest quality, but they have been included because of their historical and intrinsic interest.

Editors

The views and opinions expressed by the contributors in this book are not necessarily endorsed by the compiler and editors.

Fiducia Press publishes titles on local history, transport, music, poetry and other subjects of special interest in the Bristol and surrounding areas.

Current titles include 'Past Bristol Times', a collection of studies of Bristol's colourful past and 'Pirates and Privateers out of Bristol', describing the city's major involvement in the era of buccaneering on the high seas.

For further information contact the publishers at 10 Fairfield Road Southville Bristol BS3 1LG or for a full list of titles visit wwwbristolbooksandpublishers.co.uk